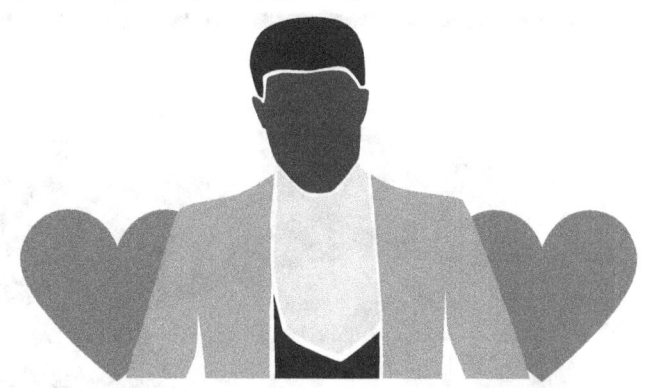

As you color each page, you can meditate on the affirmations and visualize yourself with your ideal partner. By combining the relaxing and meditative practice of coloring with the power of positive thinking, you can shift your energy towards attracting the relationship you desire.

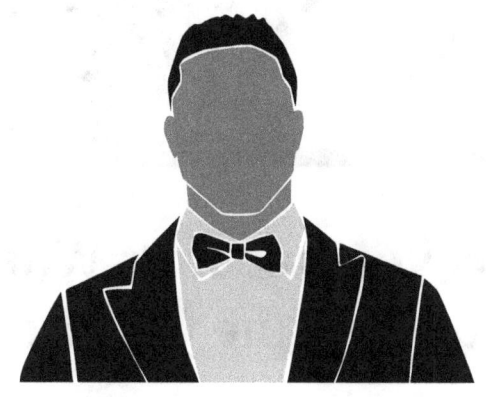

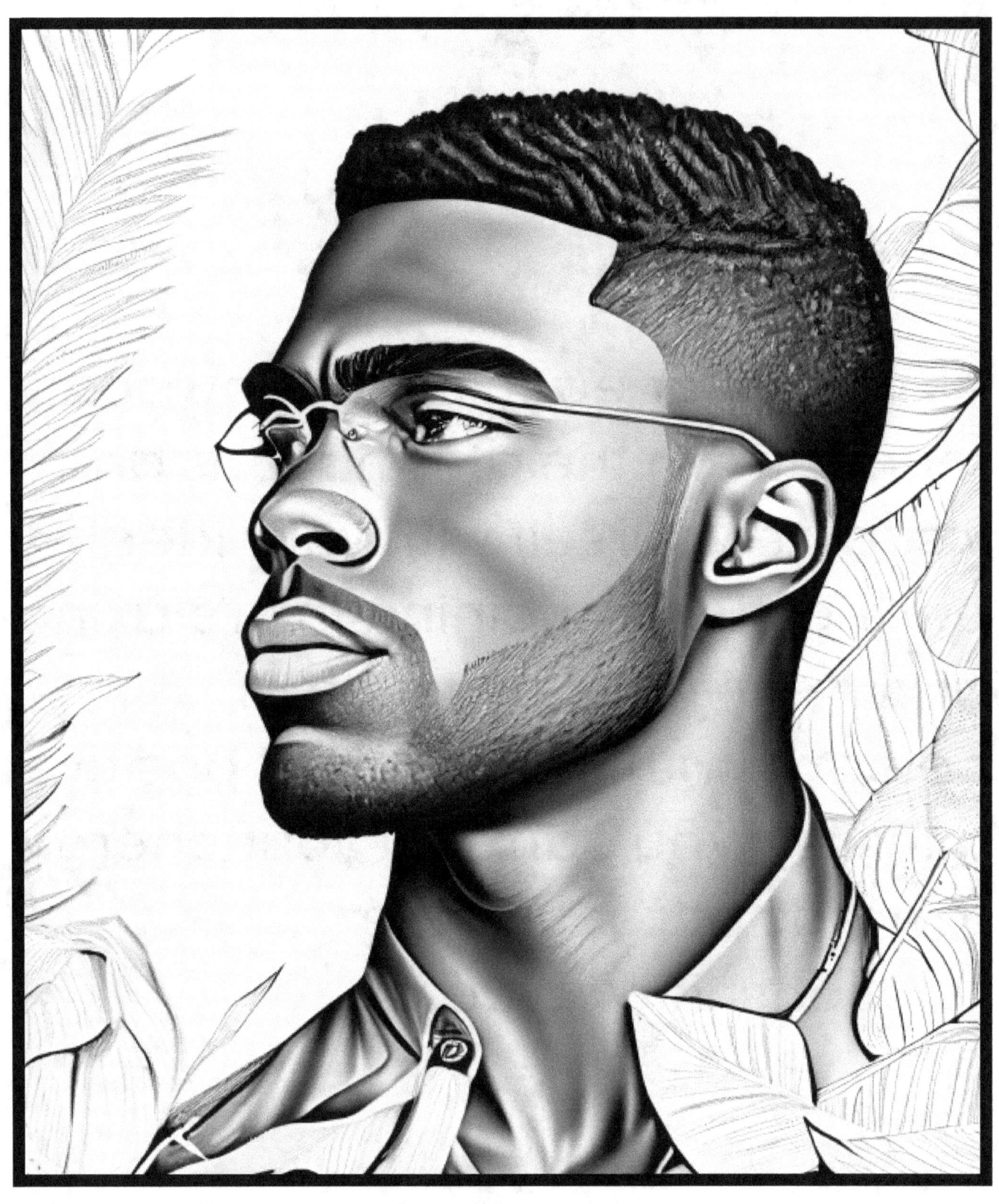

"What you think you become. What you feel you attract. What you imagine you create." —Buddha

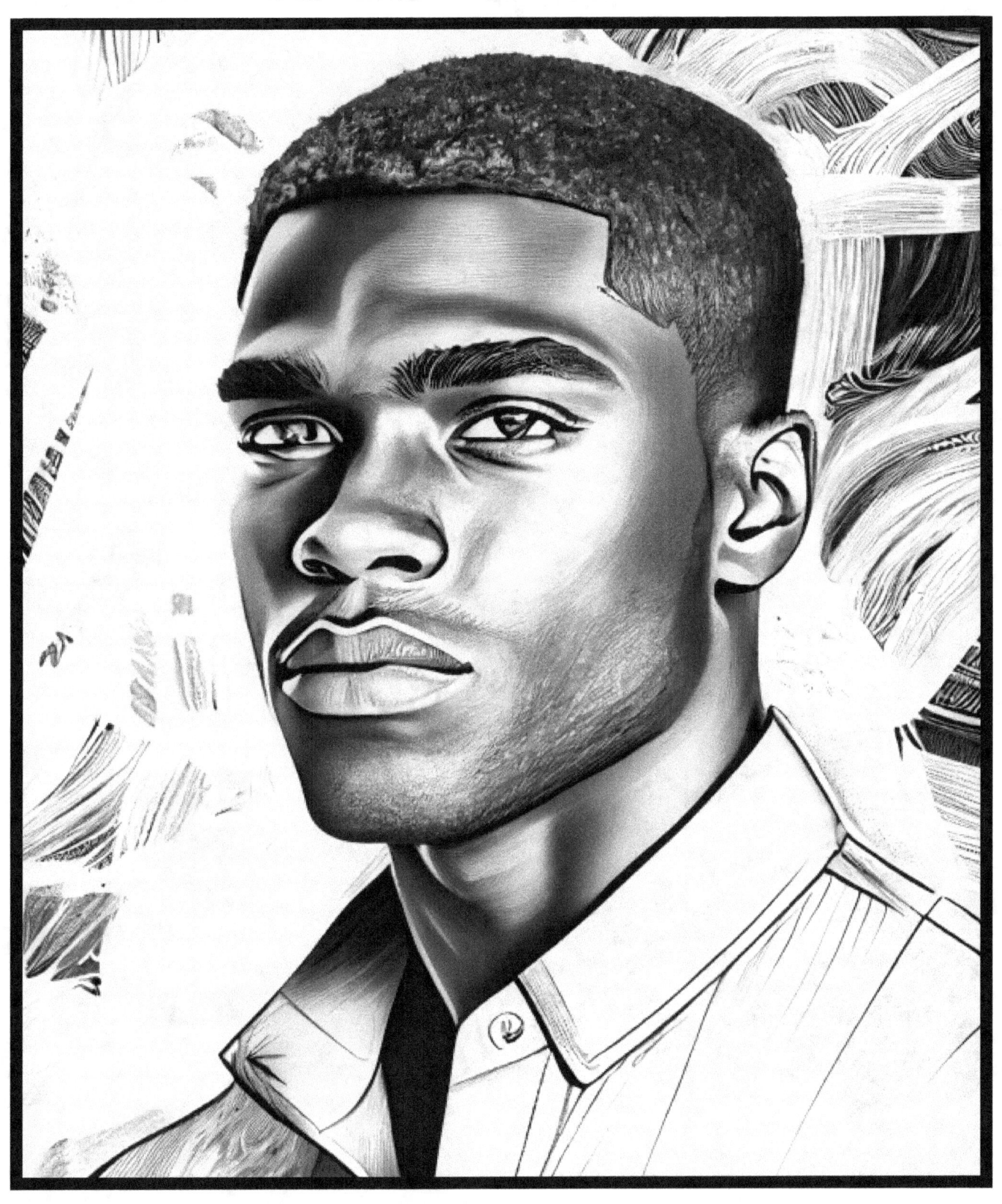

"Beware of what you set your heart upon...for it shall surely be yours." —Ralph Waldo Emerson

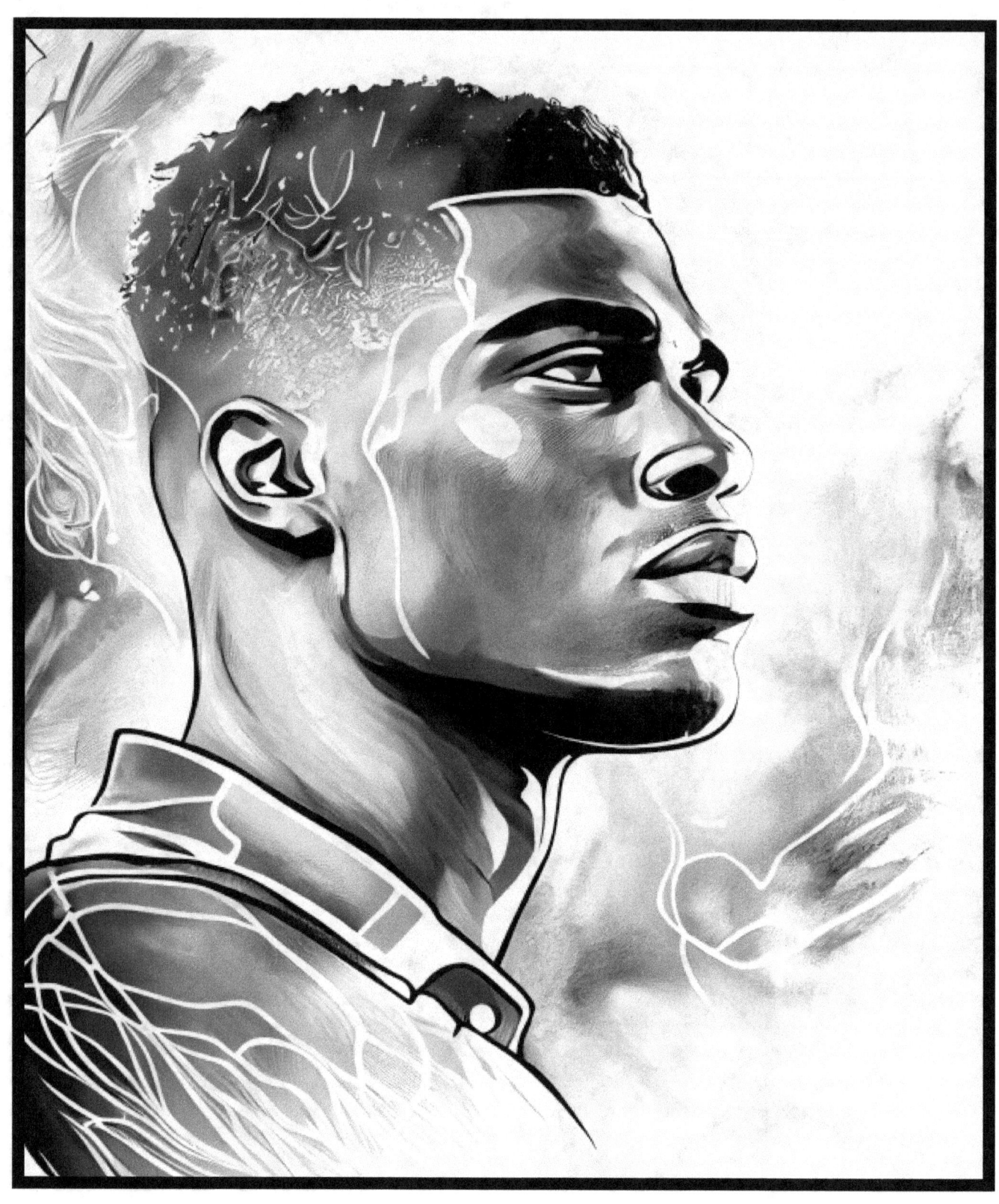

"To bring anything into your life, imagine that it's already there." —Richard Bach

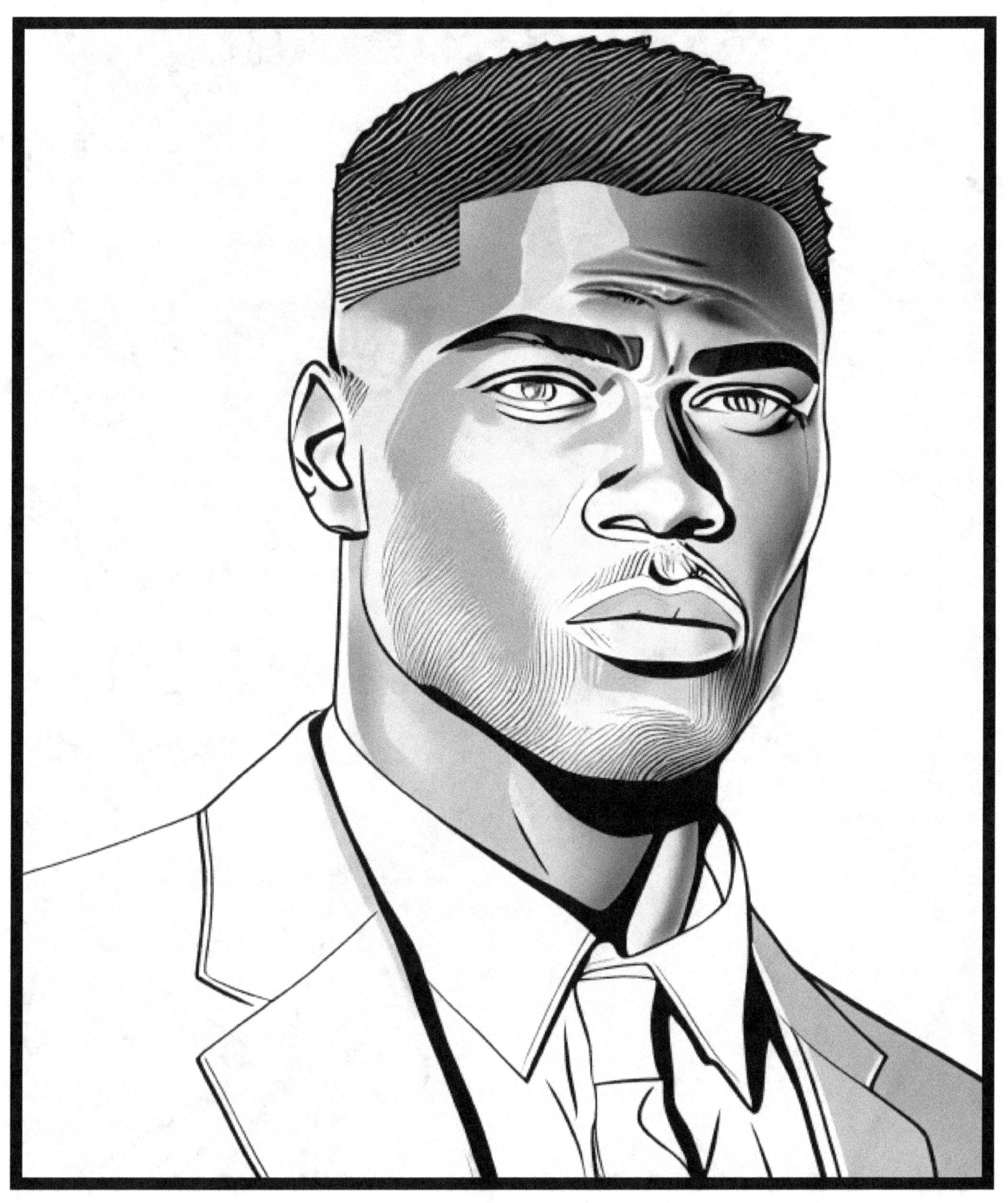

"There is nothing you cannot have. There are no limitations."

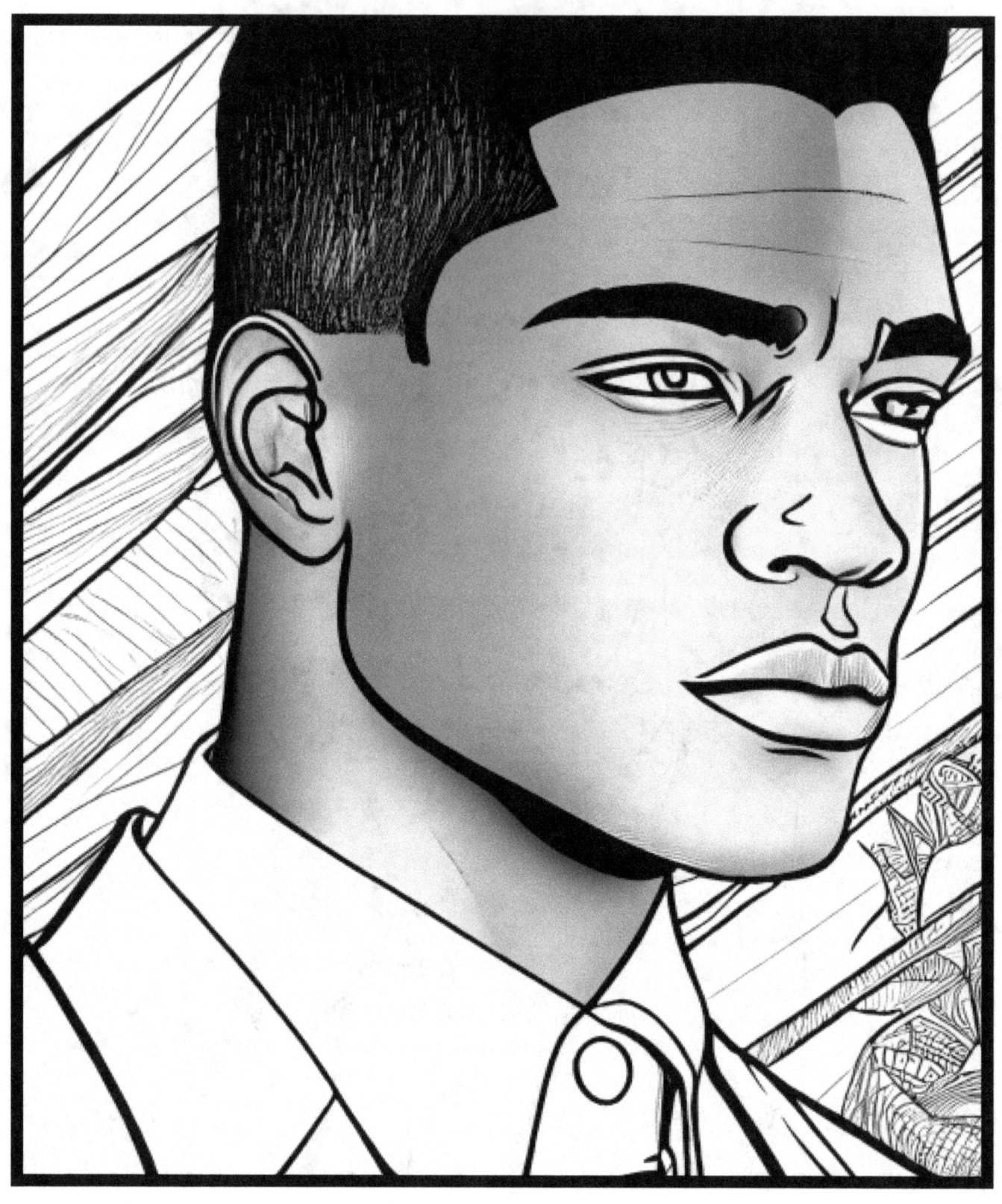

"Have faith in the magic and miracles of life, for only those that do get to experience them." —Hal Elrod

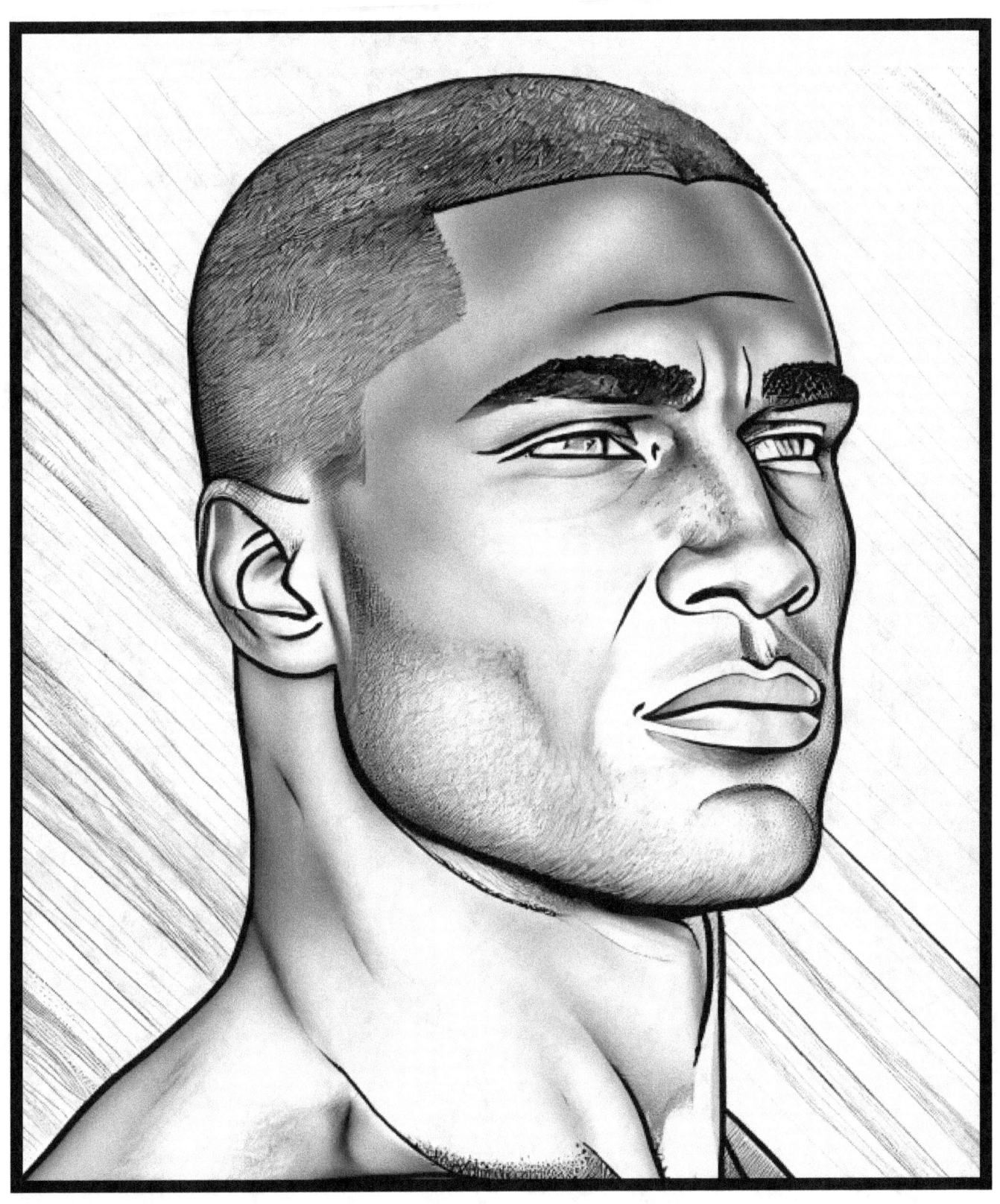

When you visualize, then you materialize. If you've been there in the mind, you'll go there in the body."
—Dr. Denis Waitley

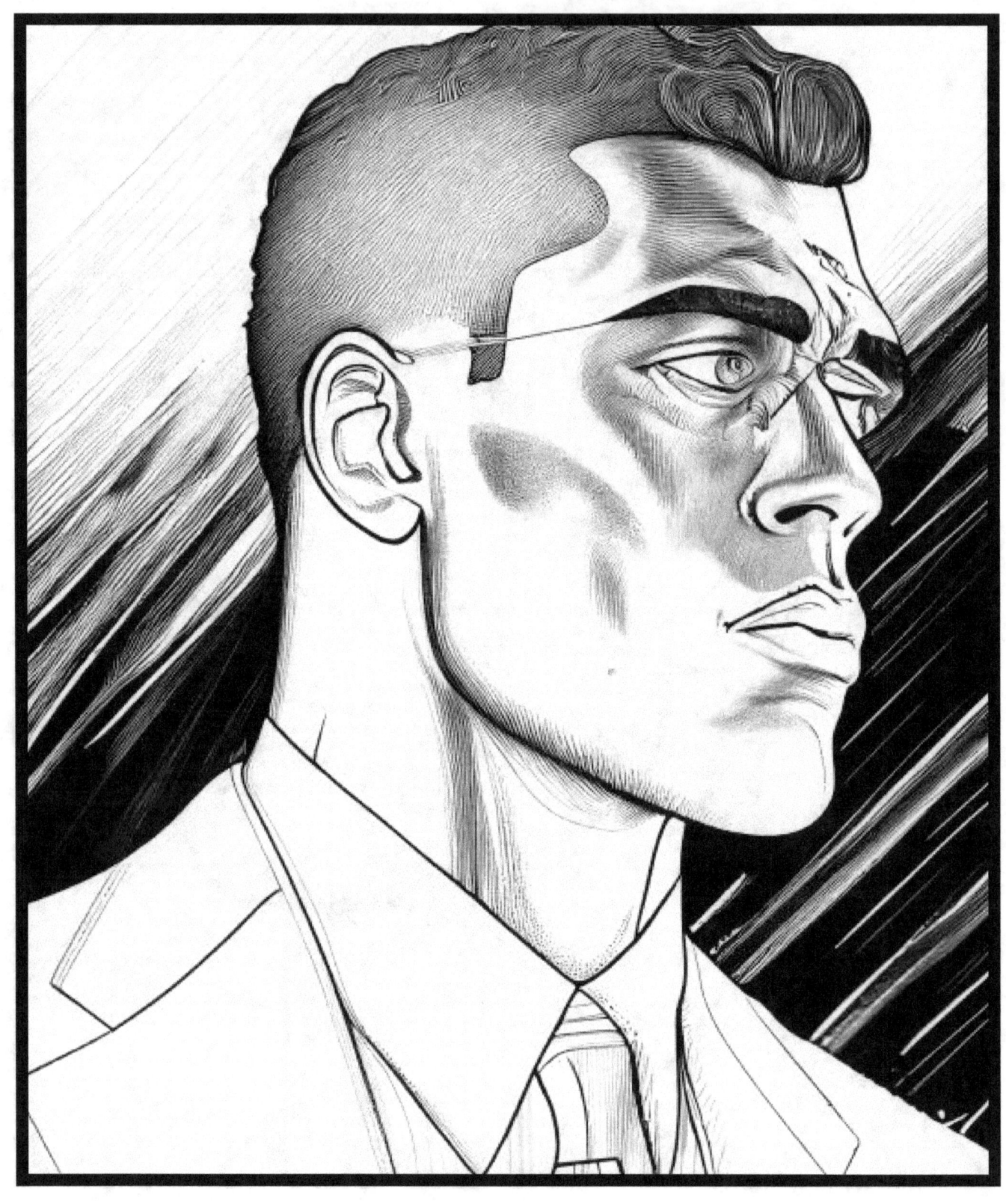

"Play the picture in your mind—focus on the end result." —Rhonda Byrne

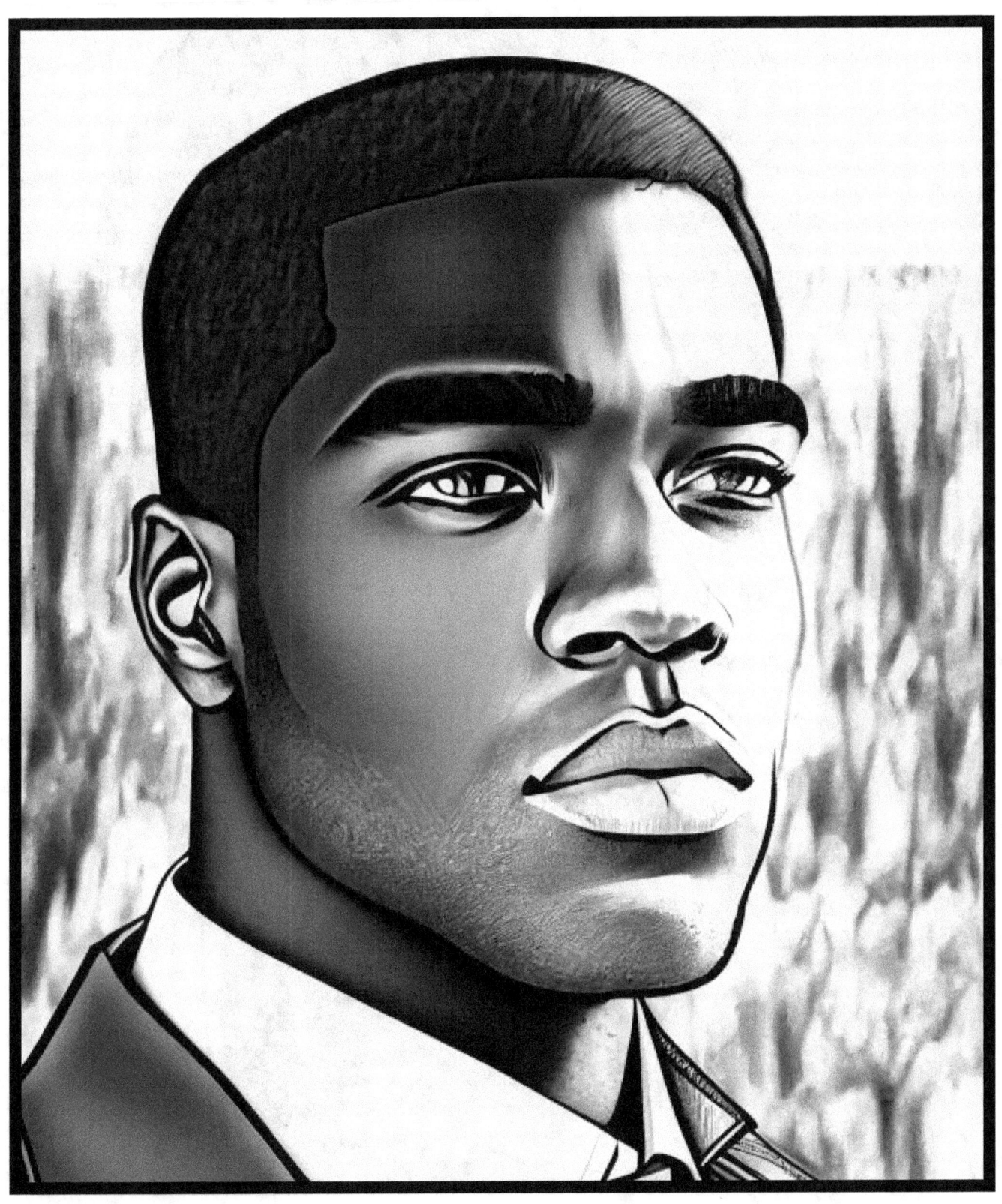

"It is the combination of thought and love which forms the irresistible force of the law of attraction."
—Charles Hammel

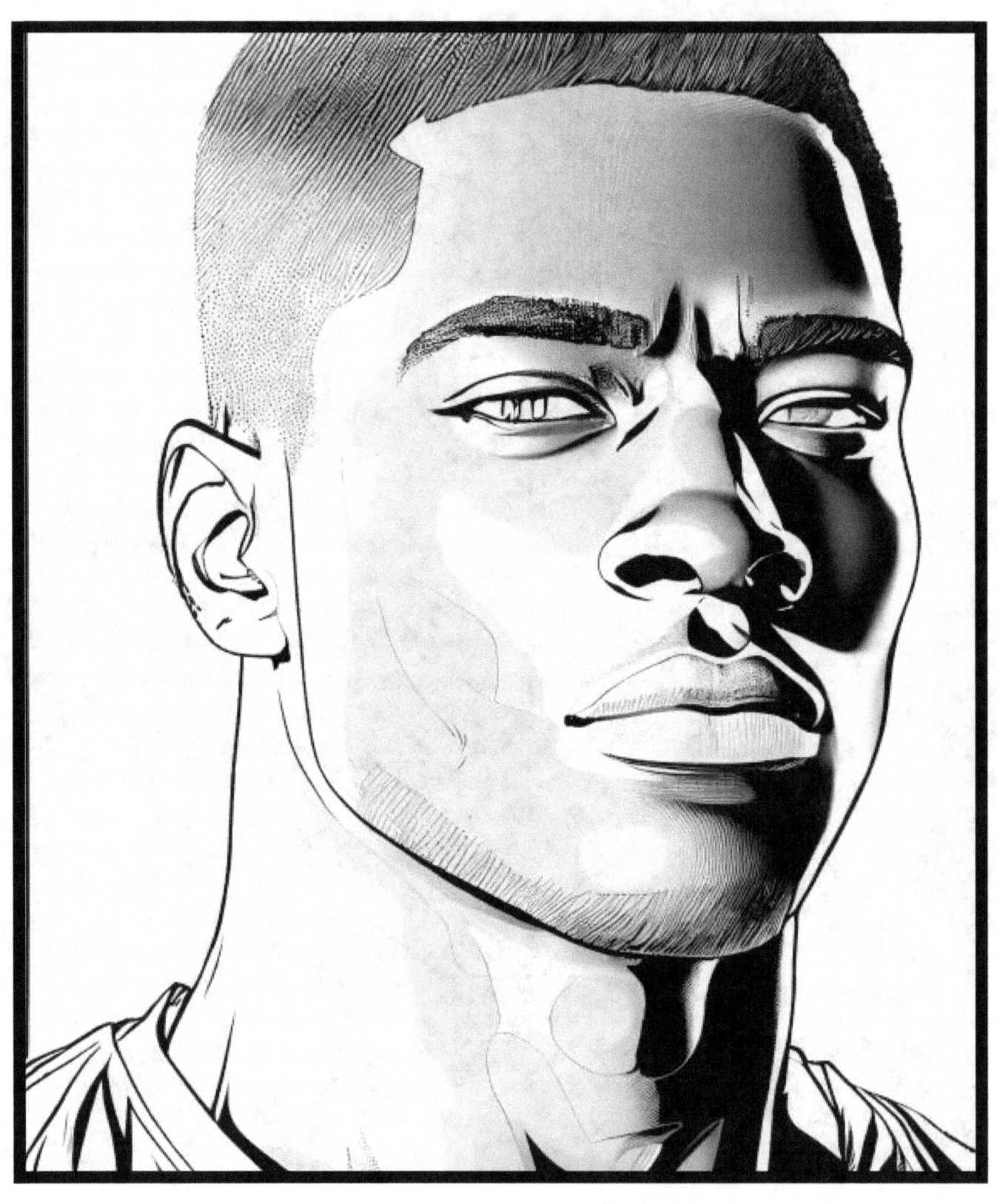

"You get in life what you have the courage to ask for." —Oprah Winfrey

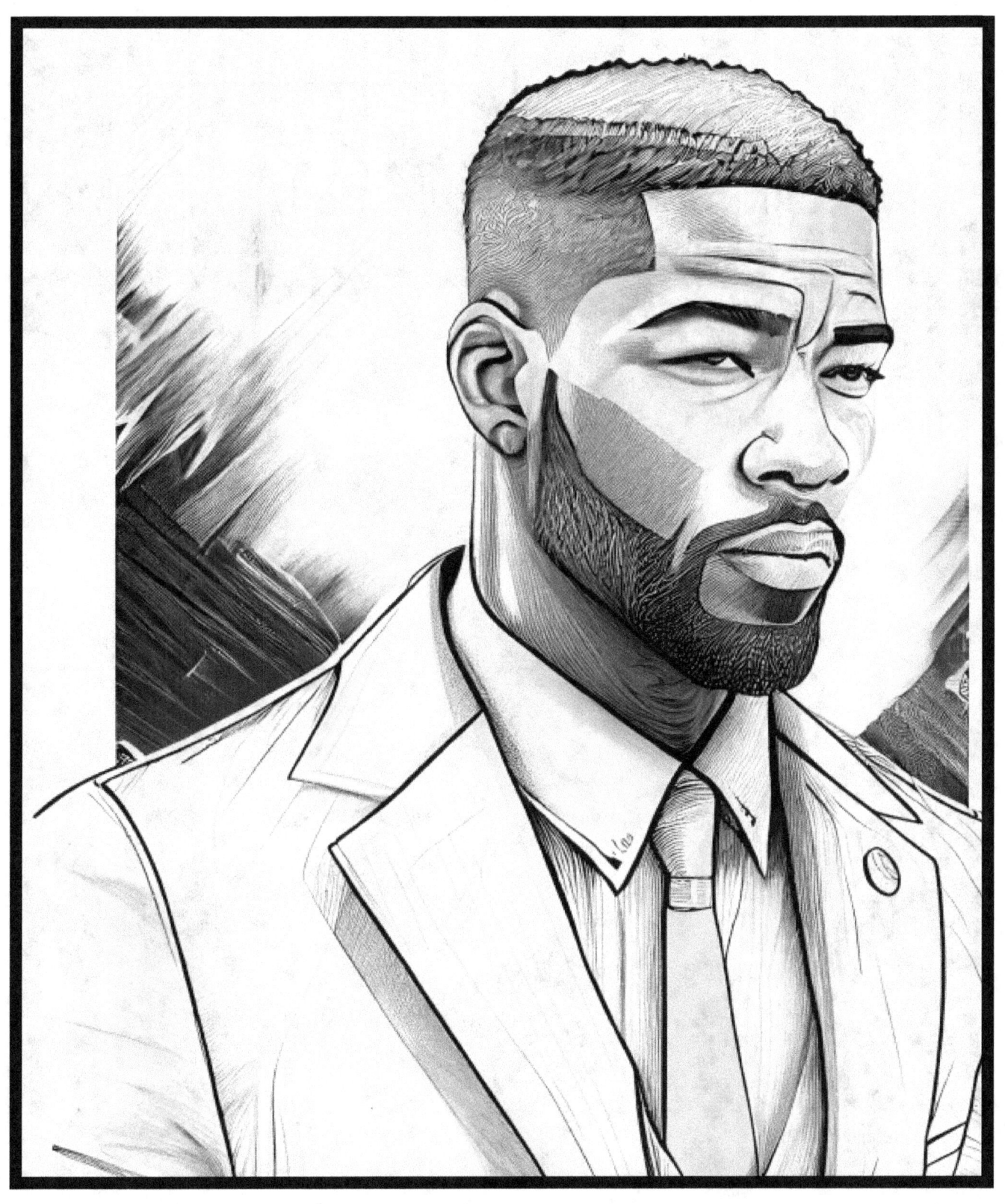

"Keep your mind fixed on what you want in life: not on what you don't want." —Napoleon Hill

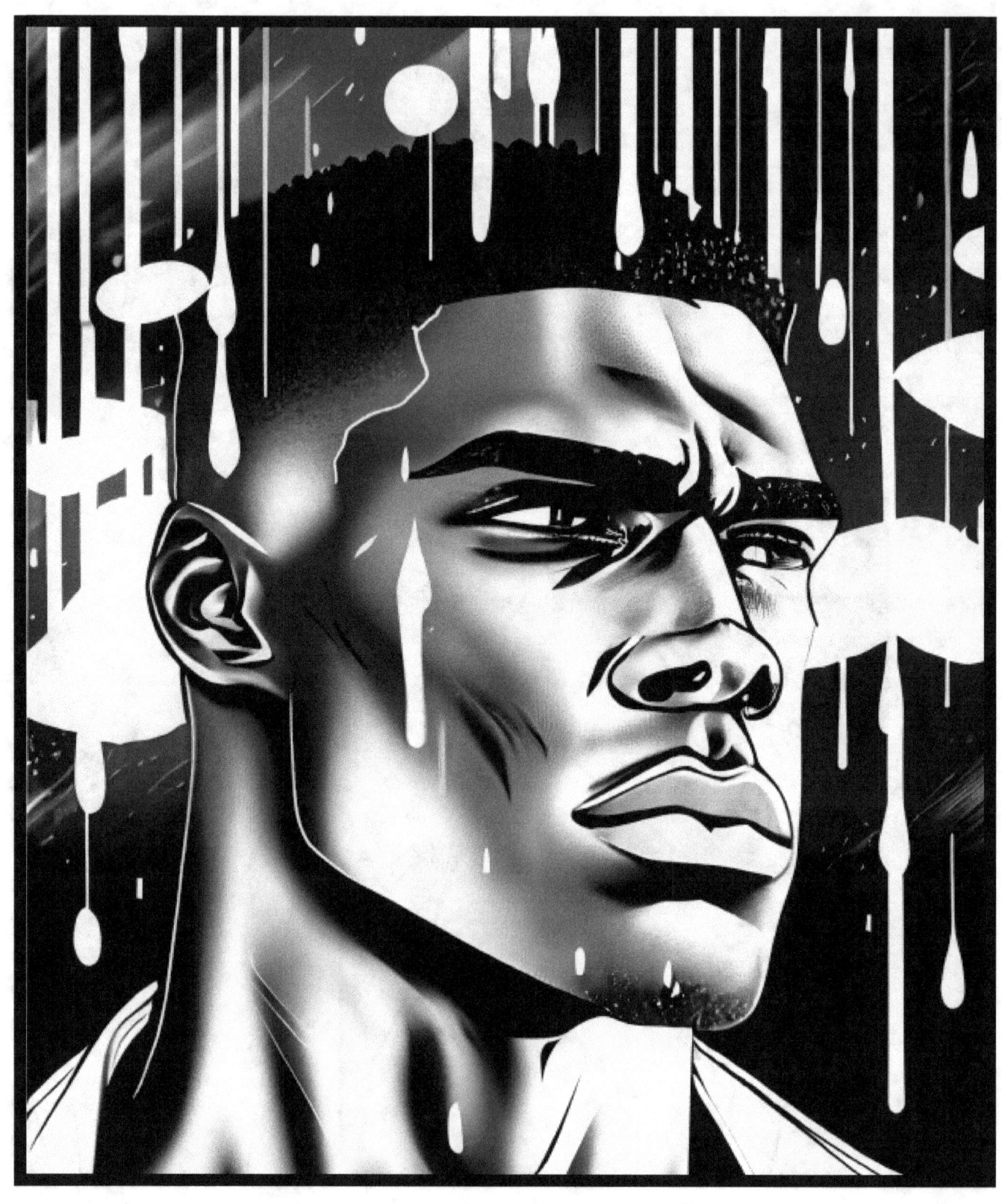

"You are in the perfect position to get there from here." —Esther Hicks

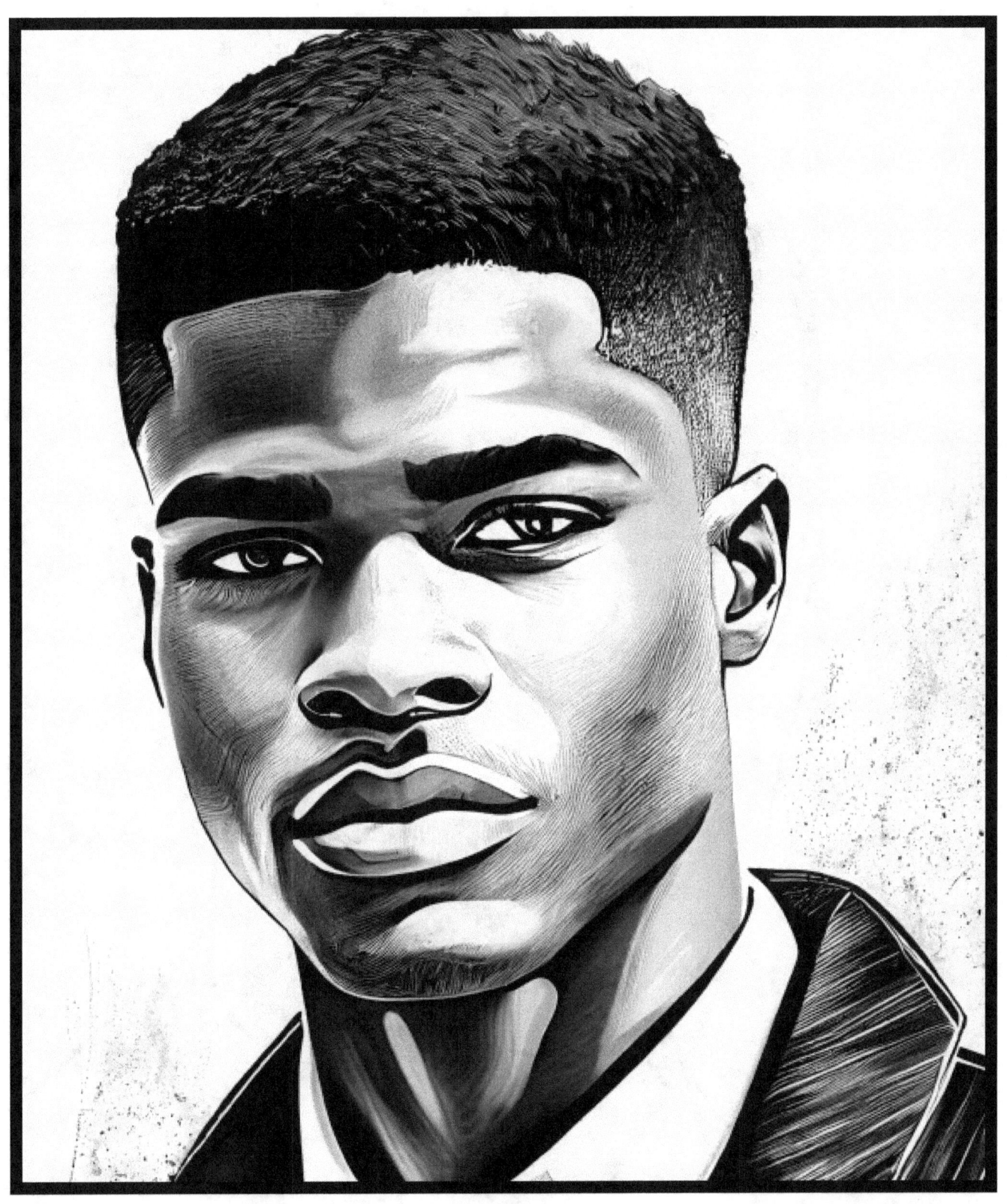

"Everything you want is out there waiting for you to ask. Everything you want also wants you. But you have to take action to get it." —Jack Canfield

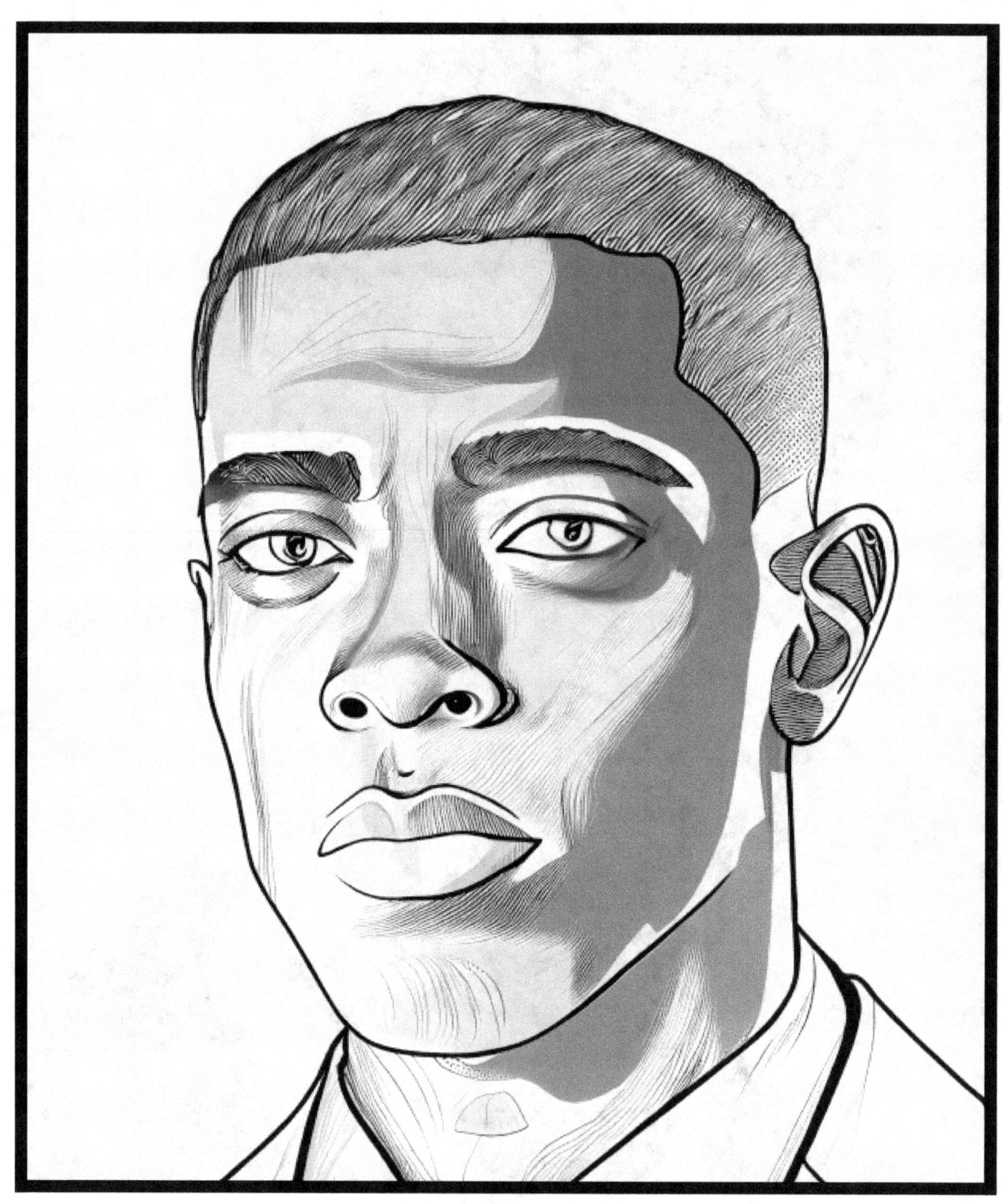

"Ask once, believe you have received, and all you have to do to receive is feel good." —Rhona Byrne

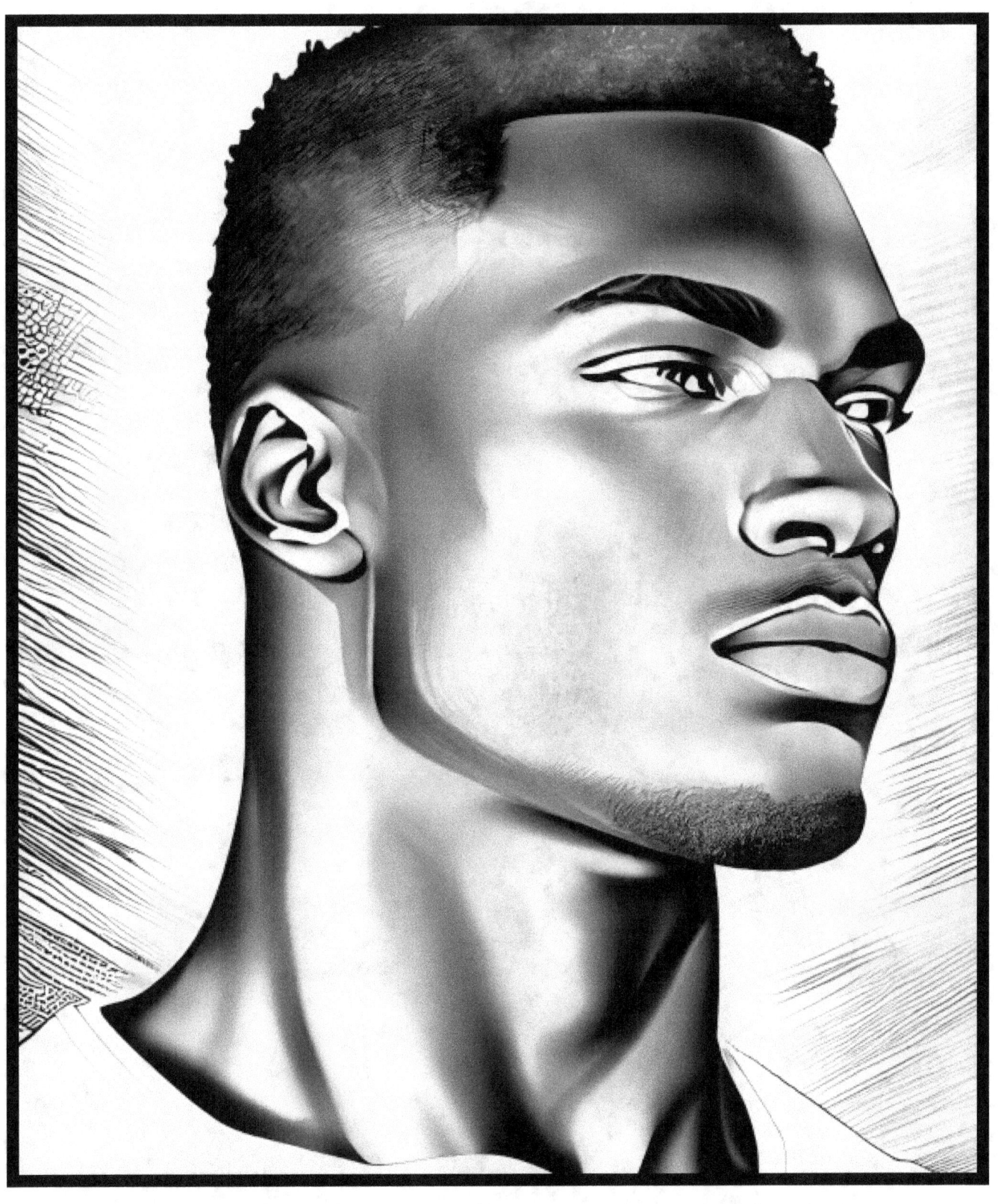

"Manifest what you want into existence by opening up to the Universe. Let it be known!"

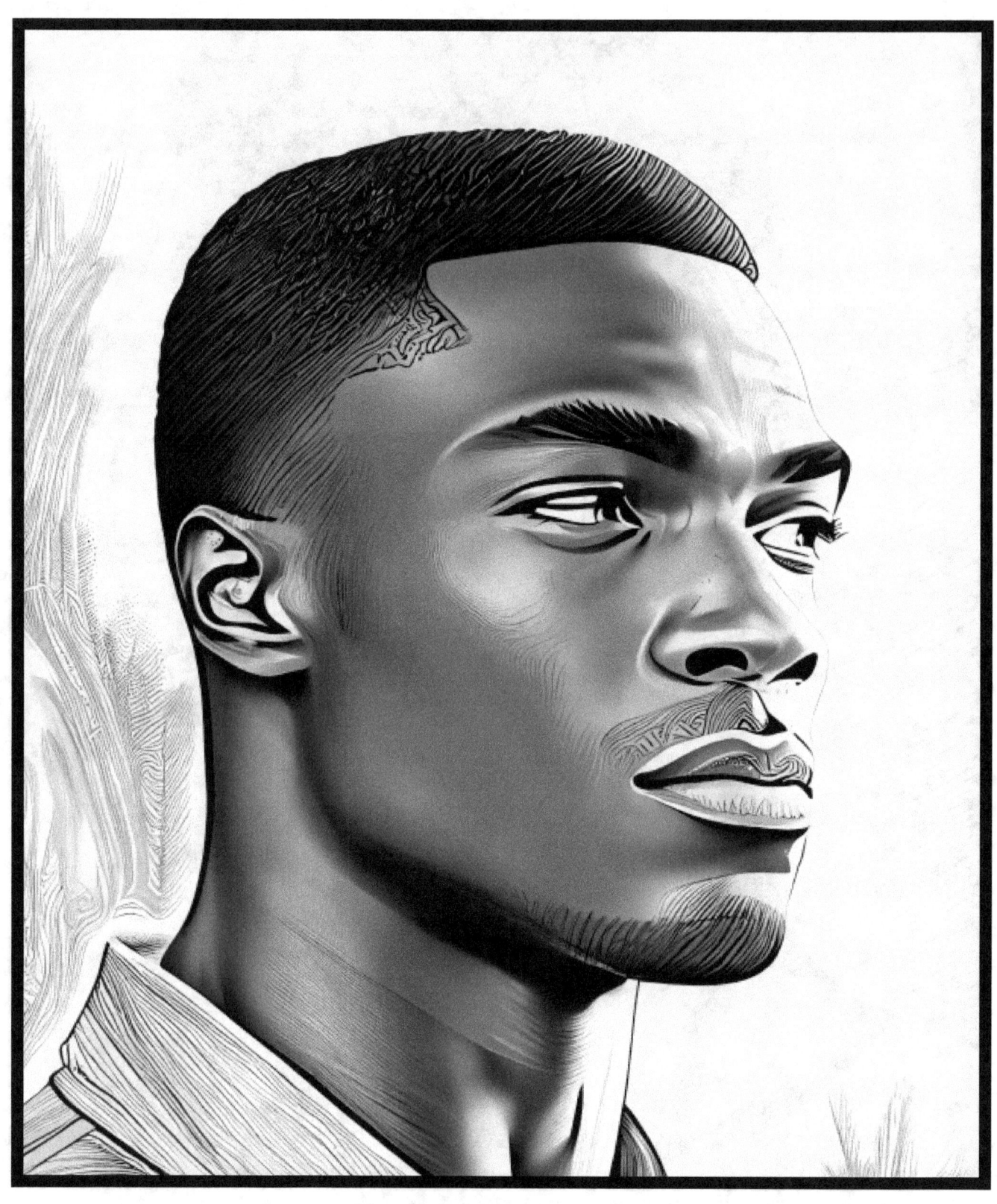

"We must radiate success before it will come to us. We must become mentally, from an attitude standpoint, the people we wish to become." —Earl Nightingale

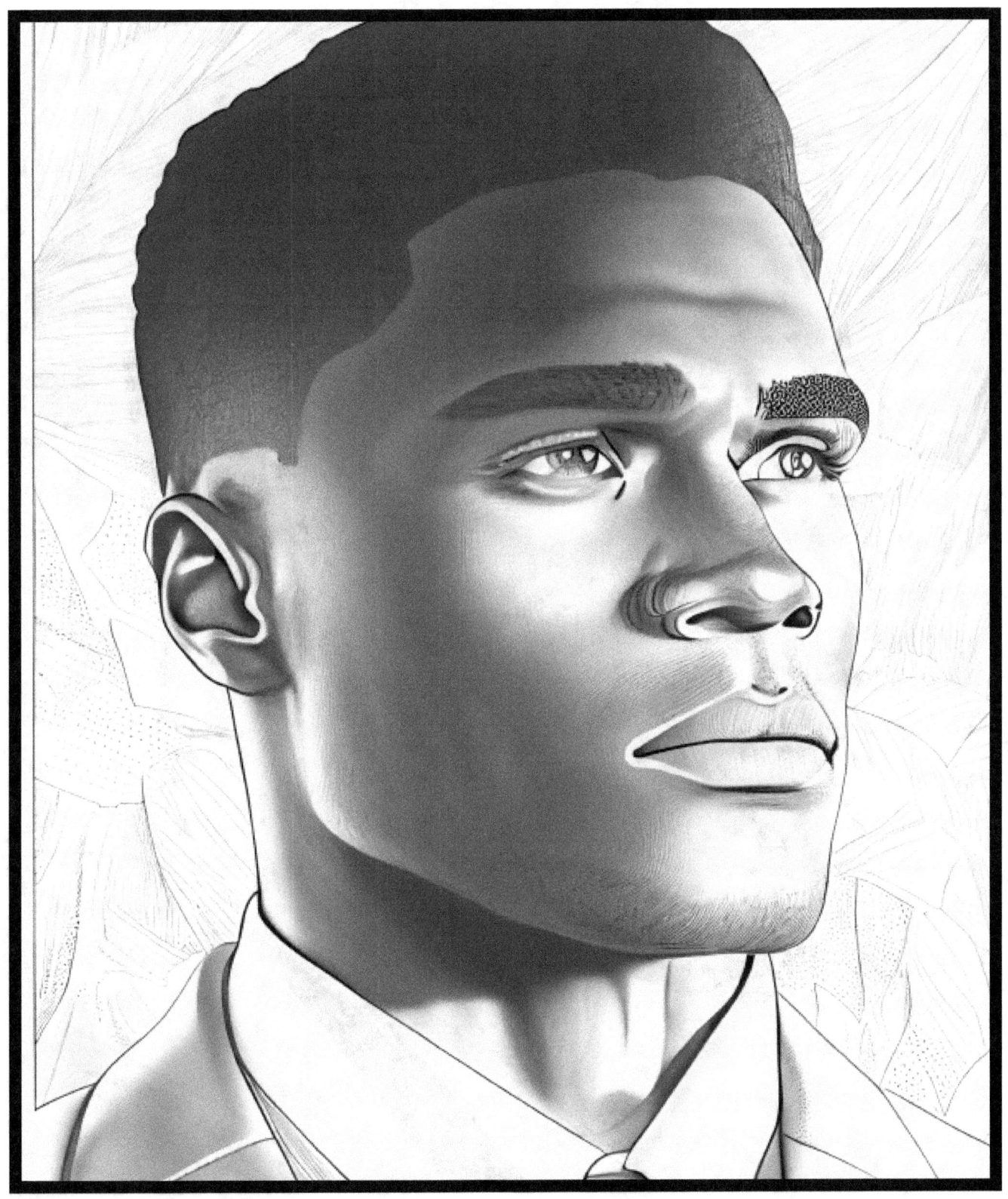

"The more you praise and celebrate your life, the more there is in life to celebrate." —Oprah Winfrey

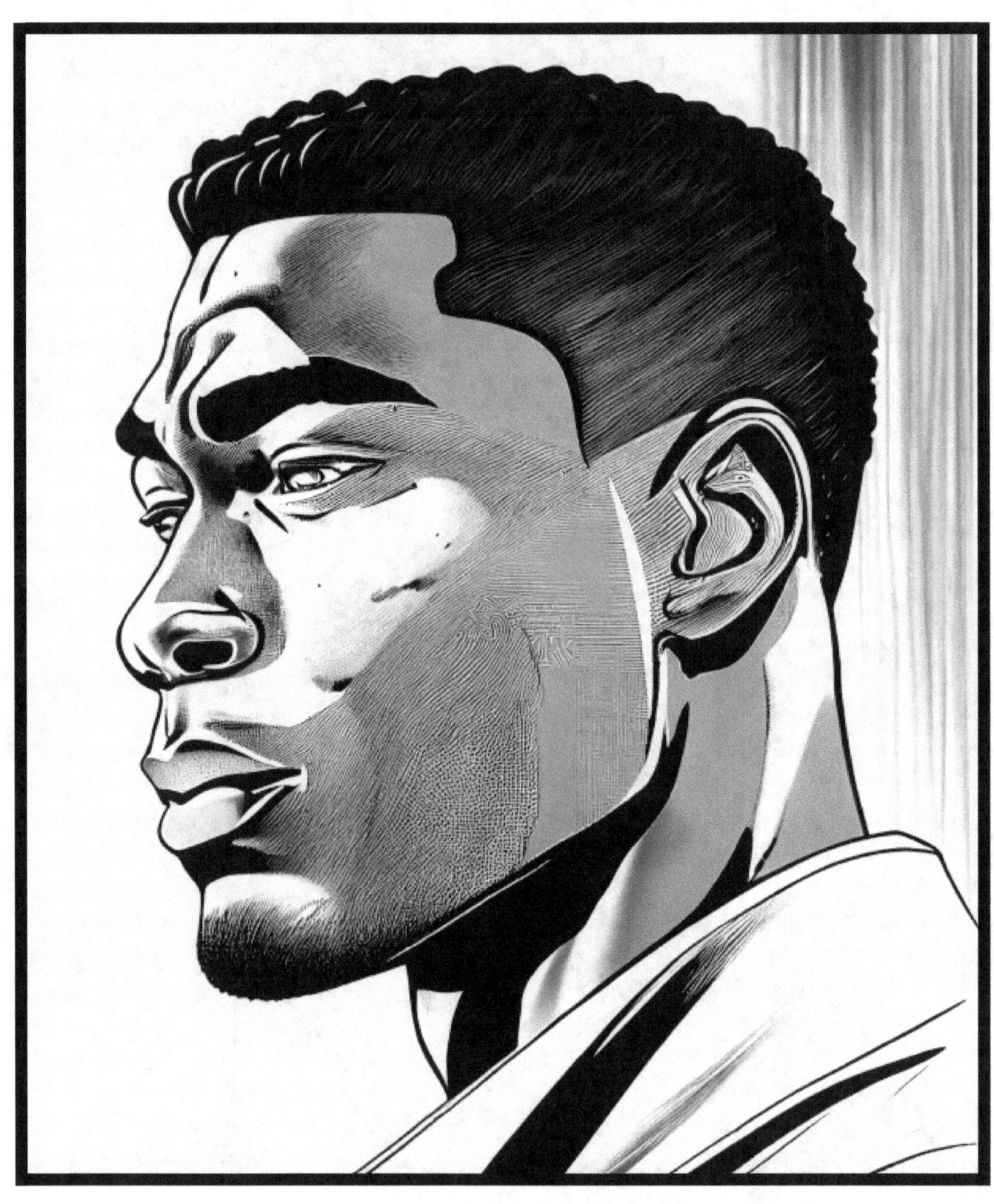

"Speak what you seek until you see what you've said."

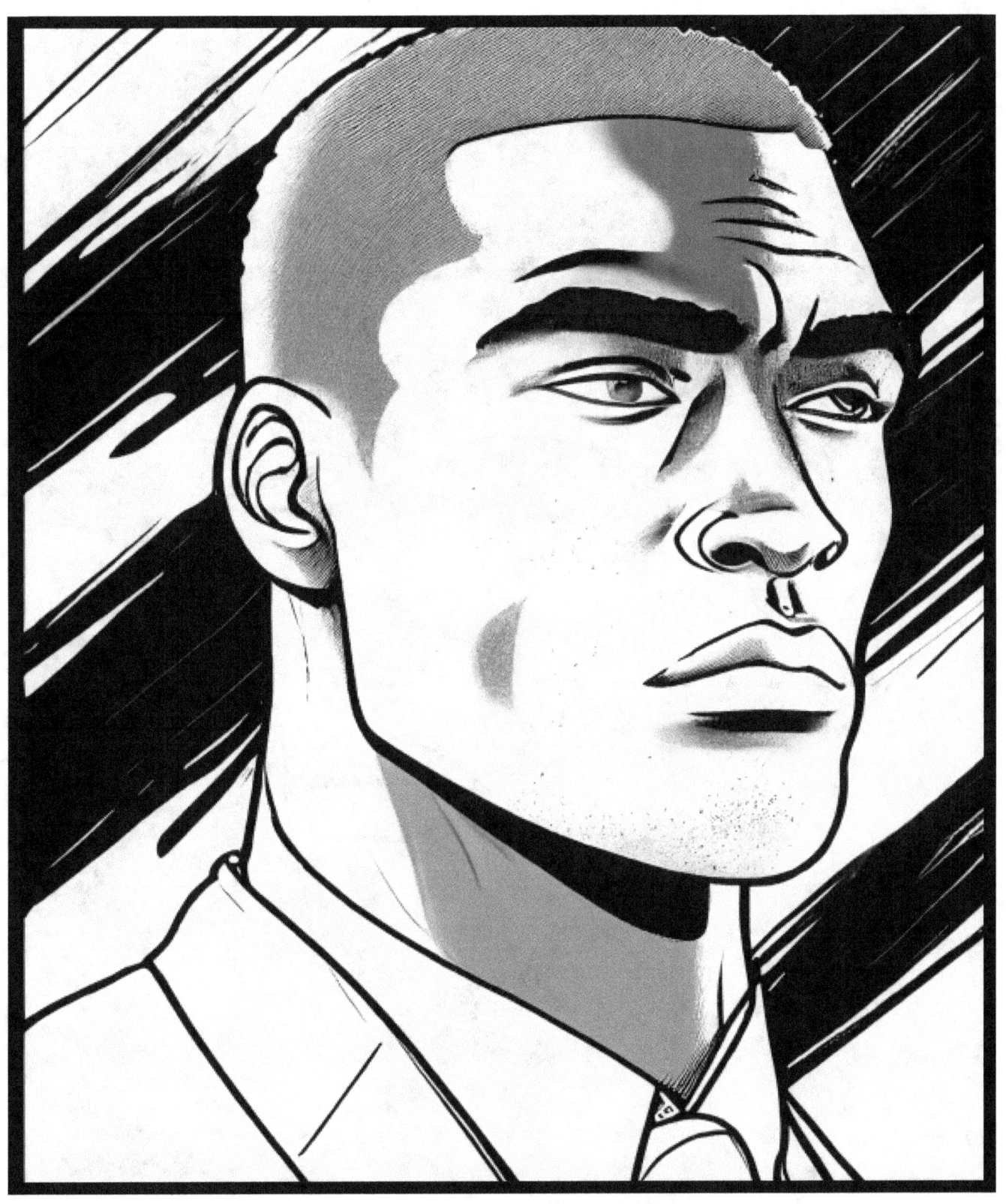

"If you want to change anything in your life, change the channel and change the frequency by changing your thoughts." —Rhonda Byrne

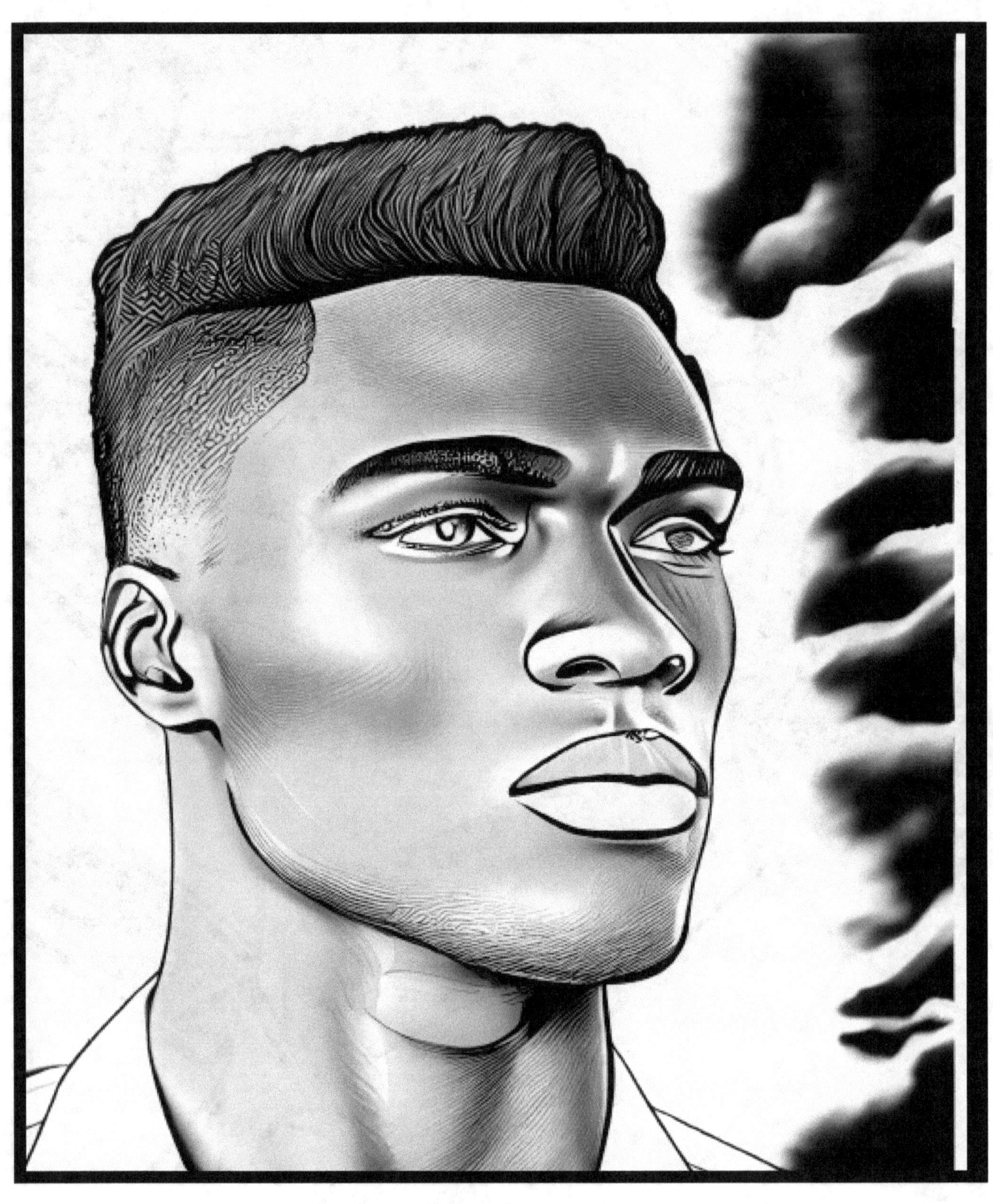

"You manifest what you believe, not what you want."
—Sonia Ricotti

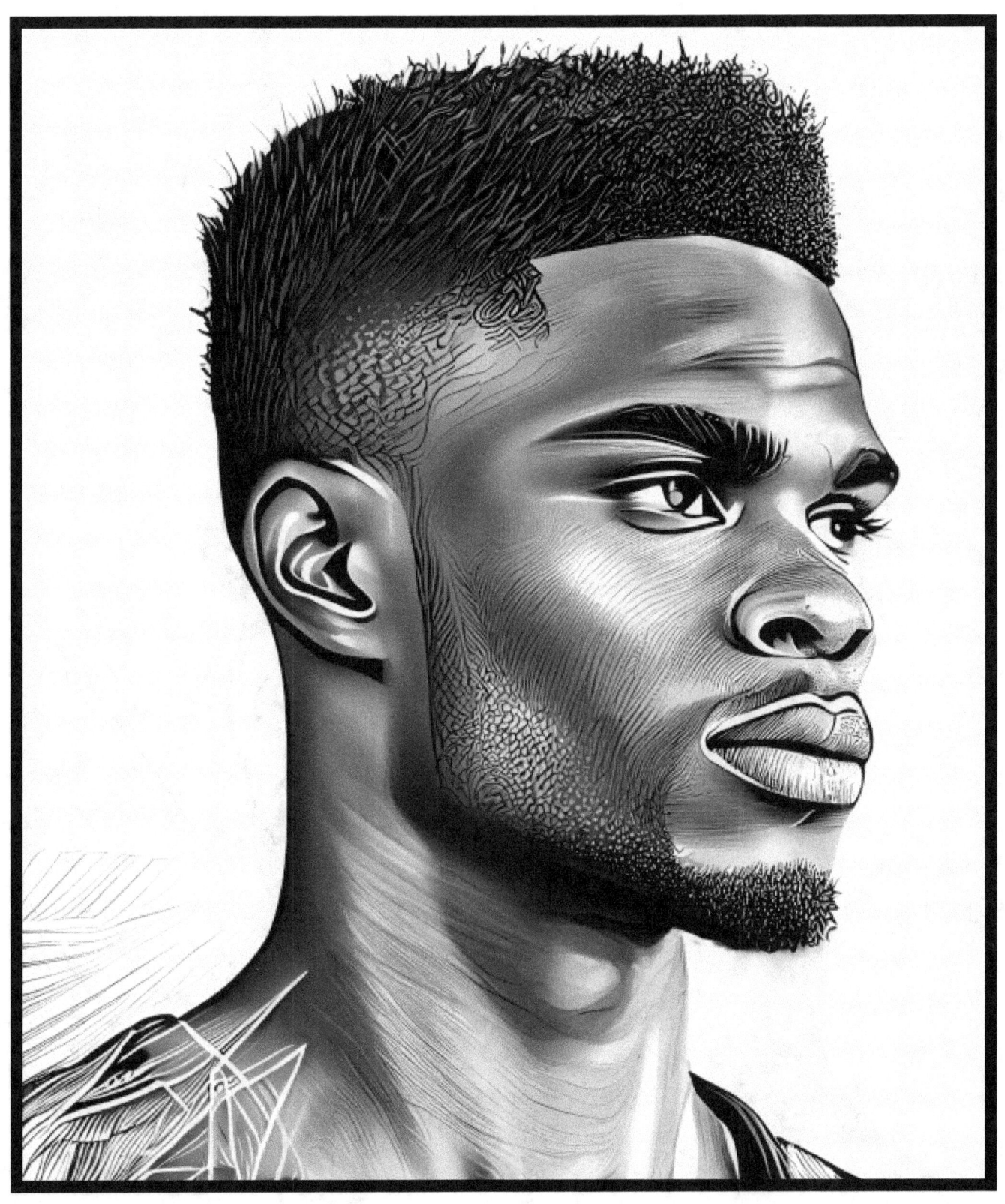

"Eliminate all doubt and replace it with the full expectation that you will receive what you are asking for." —Rhonda Byrne

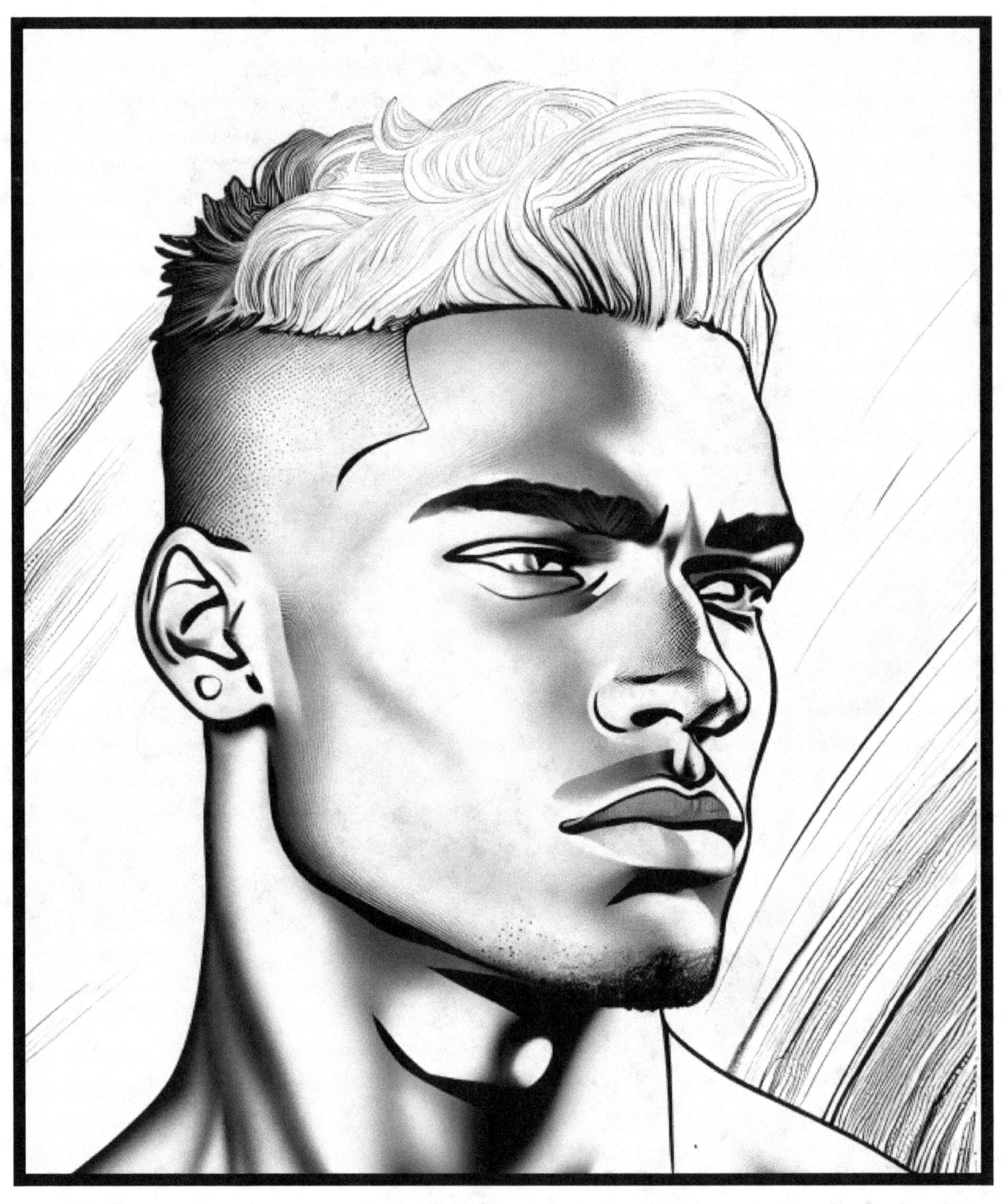

"Whatever you can do, or dream you can, begin it. Boldness has genius, power, and magic in it. Begin it now." —Johann Wolfgang von Goethe

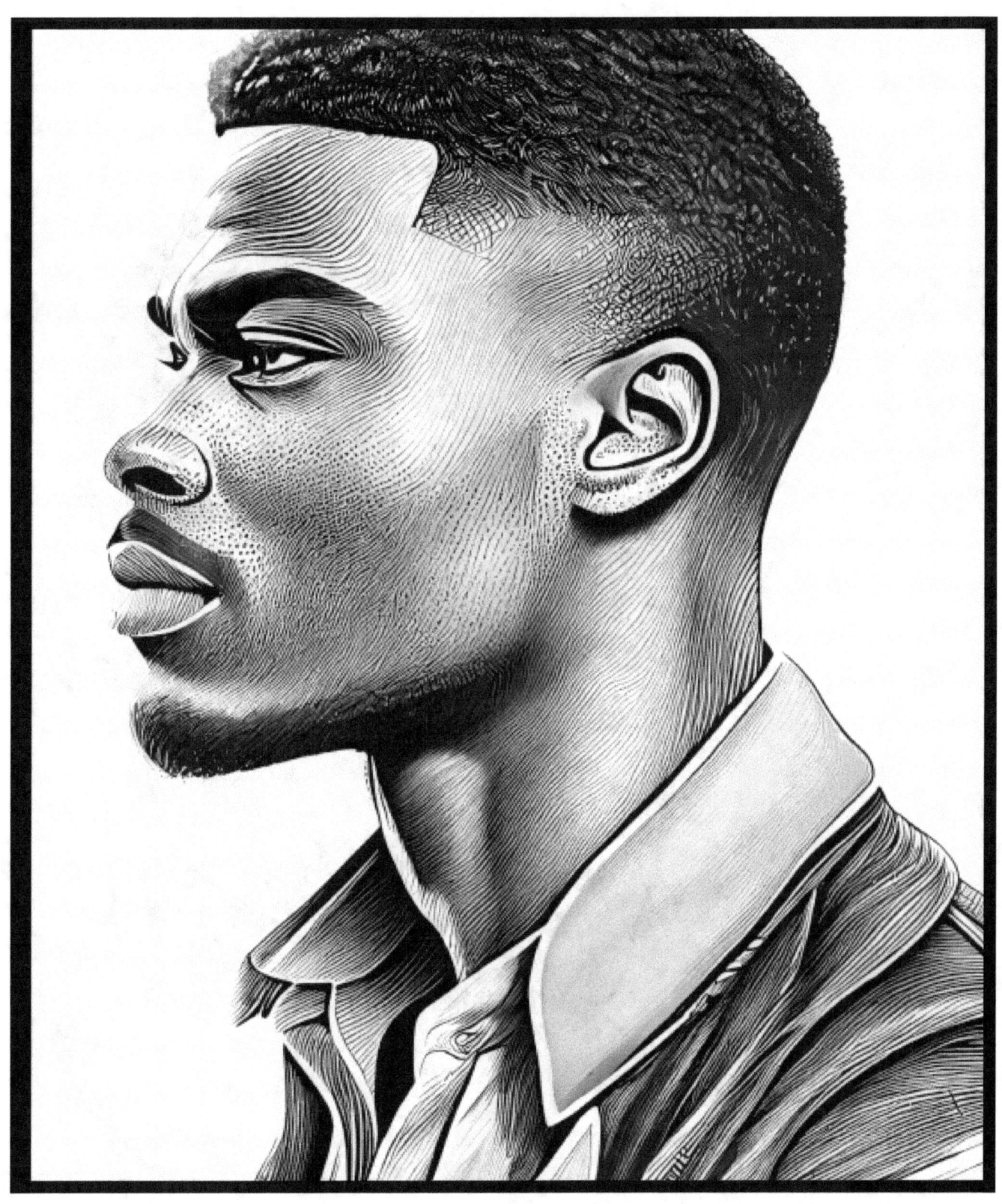

"You are the creator of your own reality."
—Esther Hicks

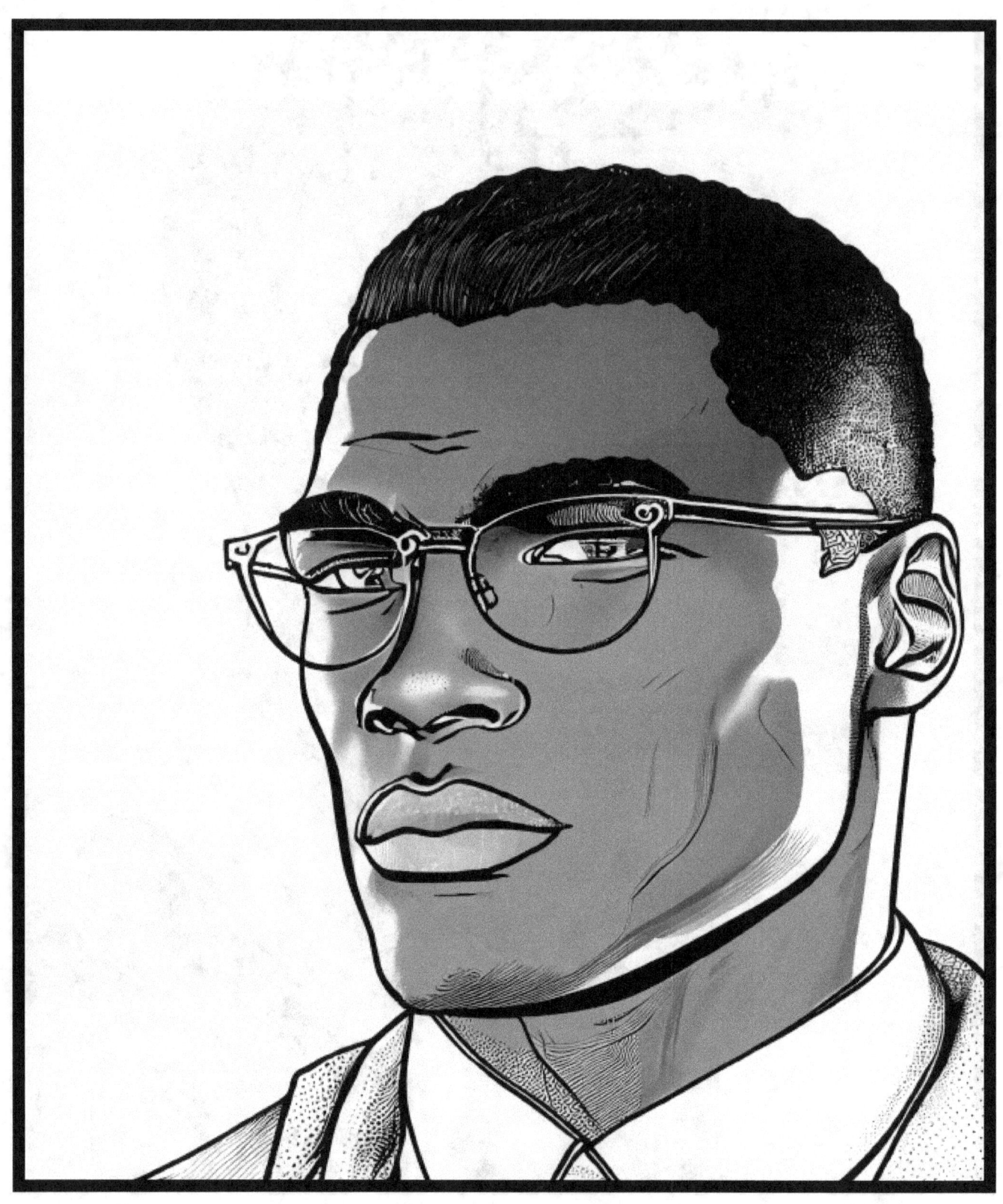

"What you radiate outward in your thoughts, feelings, mental pictures and words, you attract into your life." —Catherine Ponder

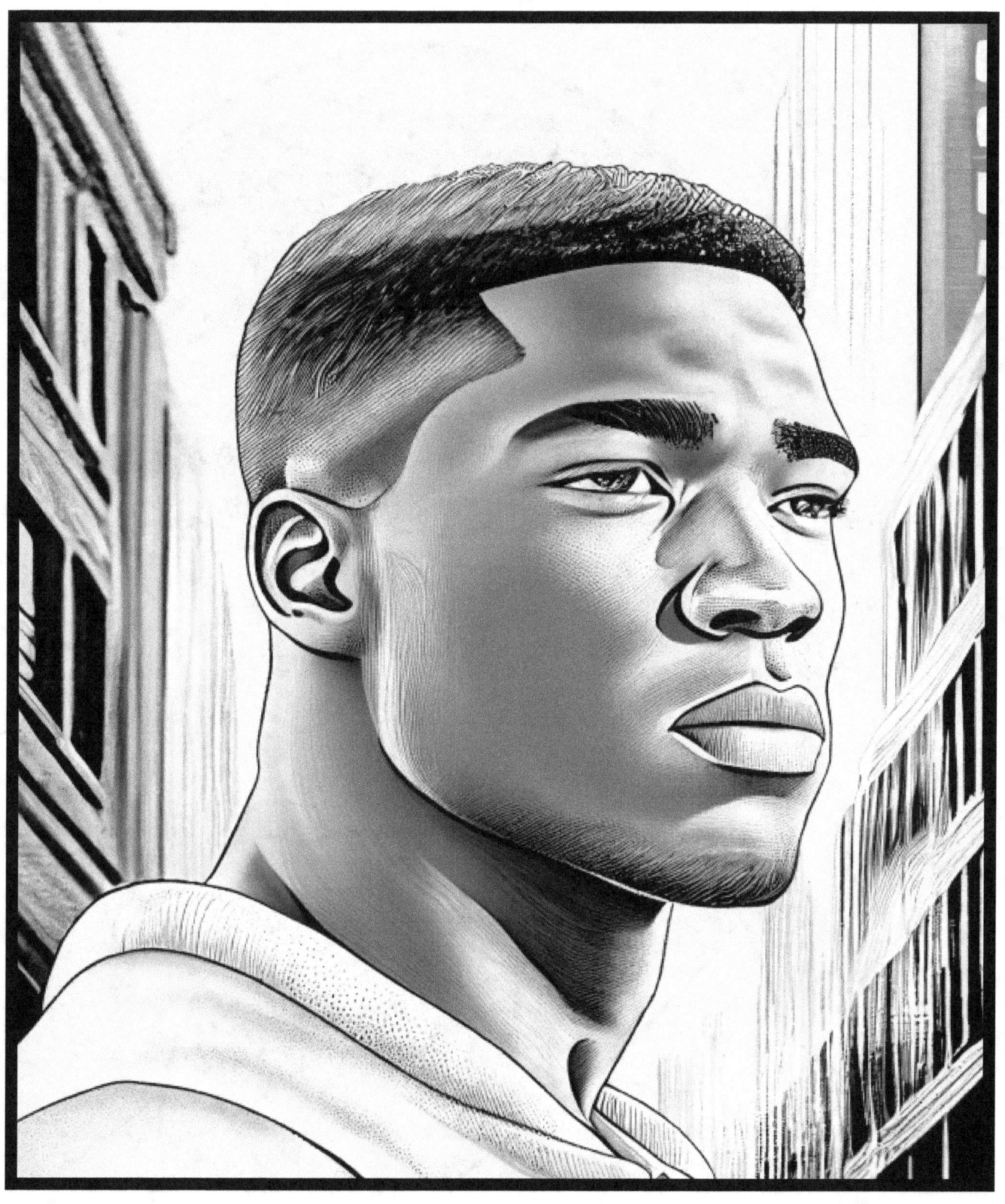

"Your whole life is a manifestation of the thoughts that go on in your head." —Lisa Nihols

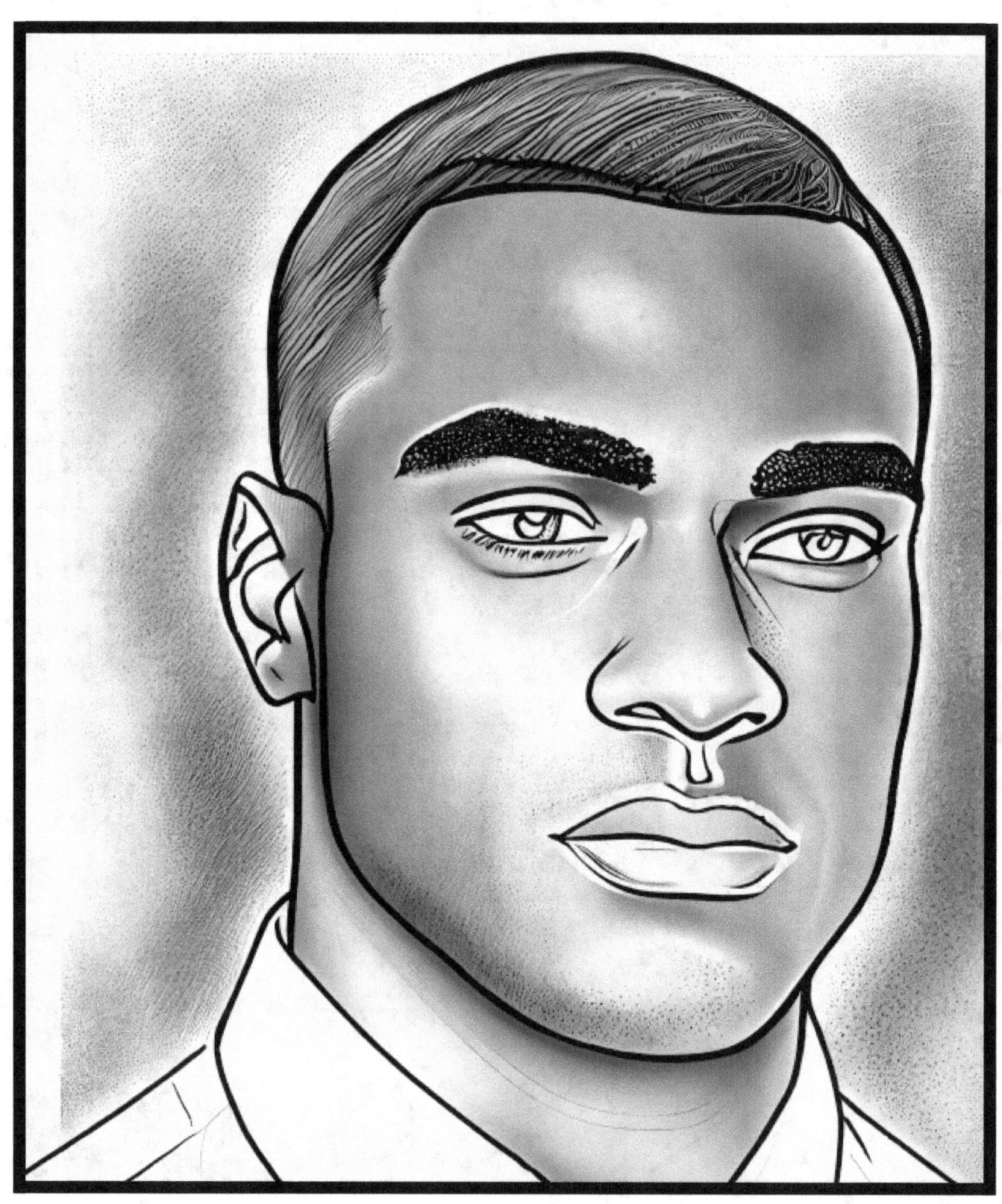

"The universe is not outside of you. Look inside yourself; everything that you want, you already are."
—Rumi

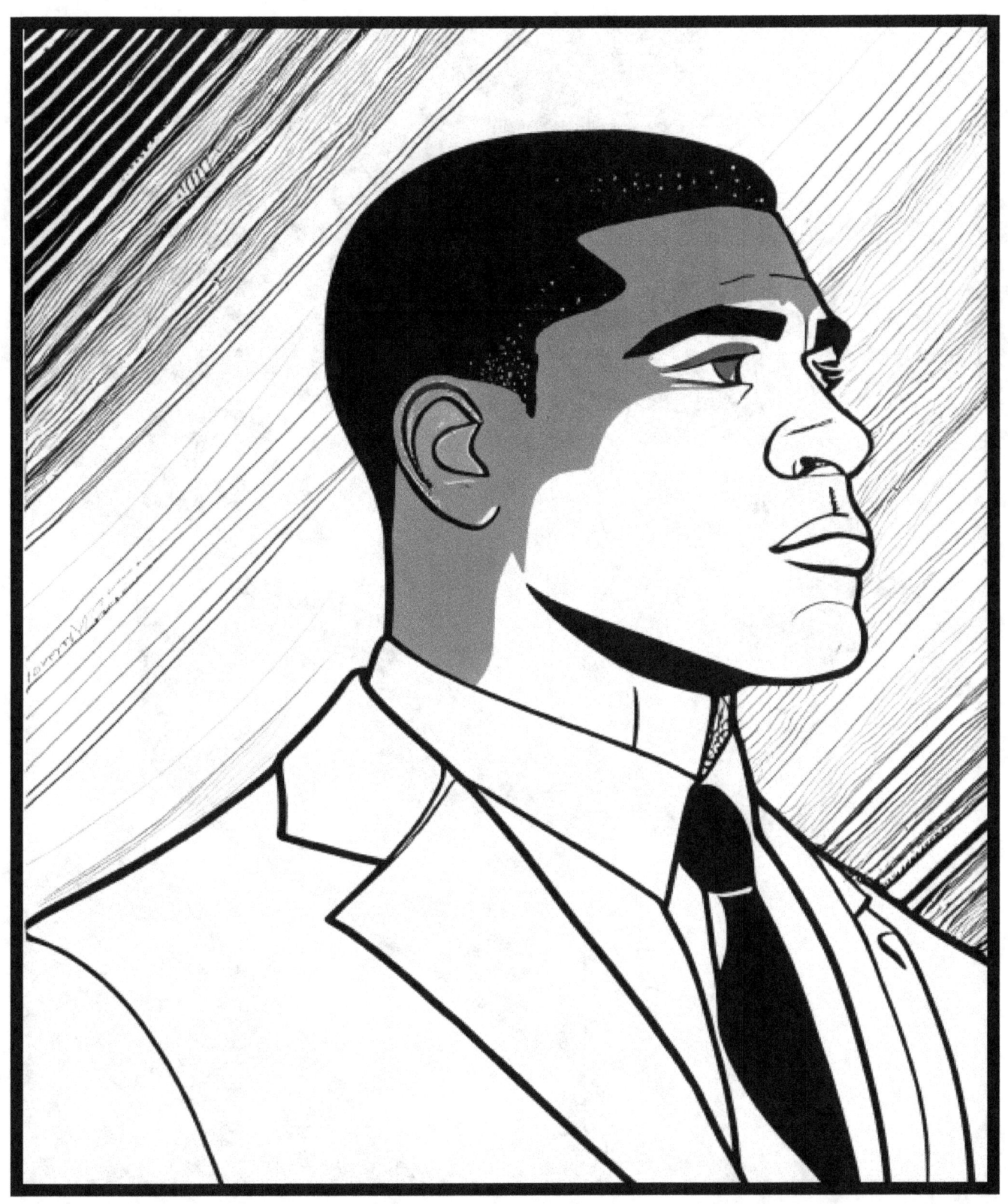

"Every intention sets energy into motion, whether you are aware of it or not." —Henry David Thoreau

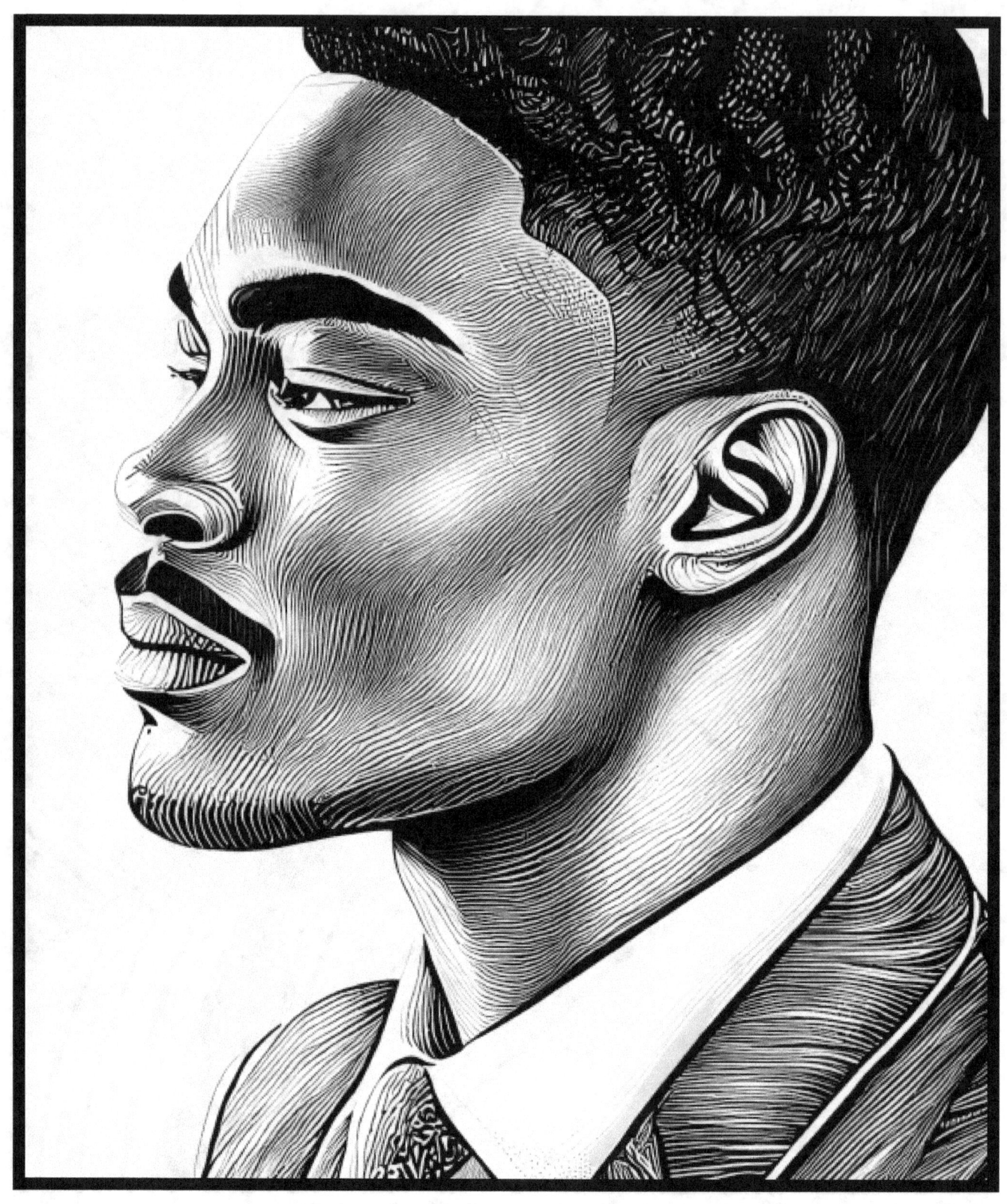

"You already have within you everything you need to turn your dreams into reality."
—Wallace D. Wattles

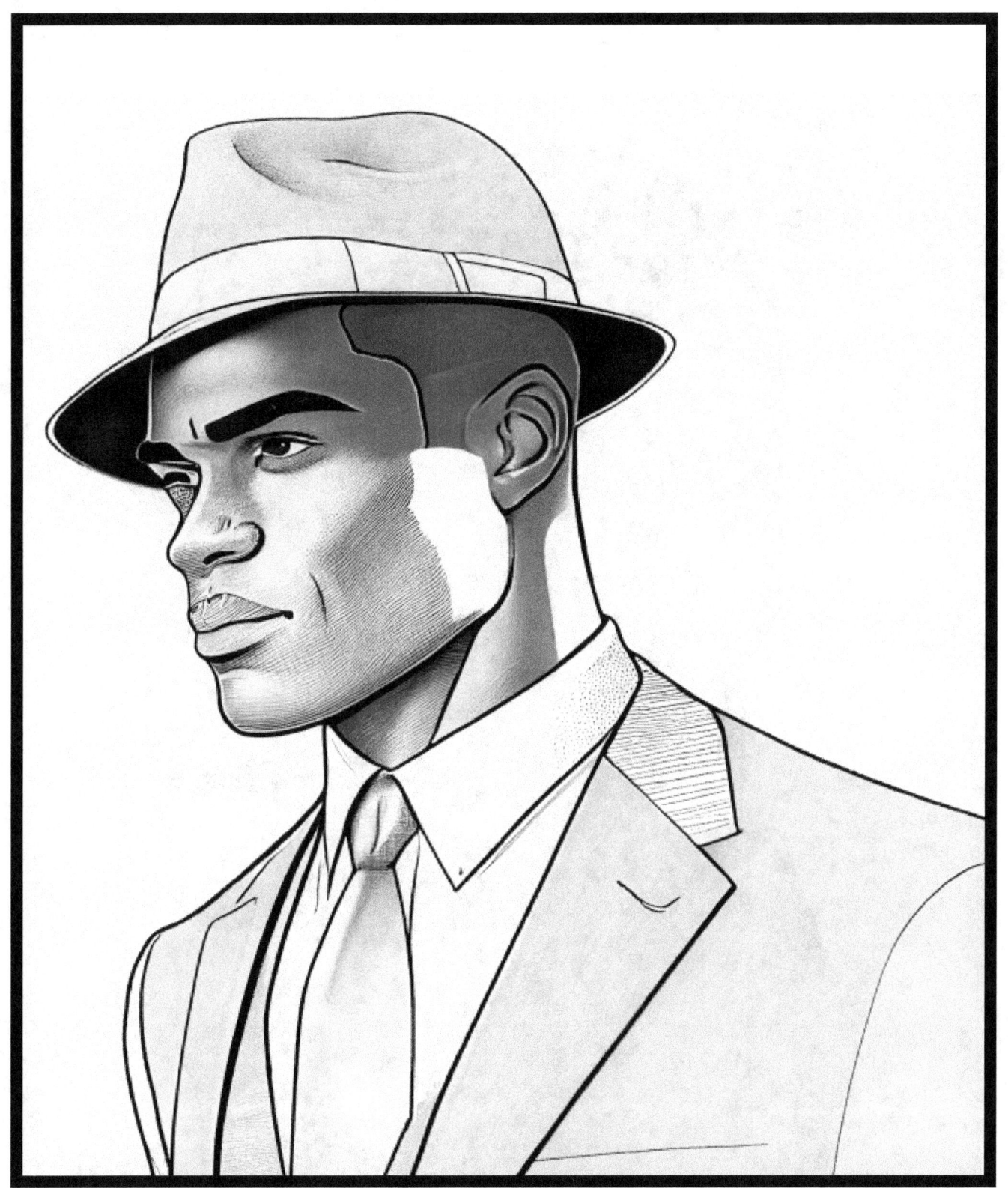

"You become what you think about most, but you also attract what you think about most."
—John Assaraf

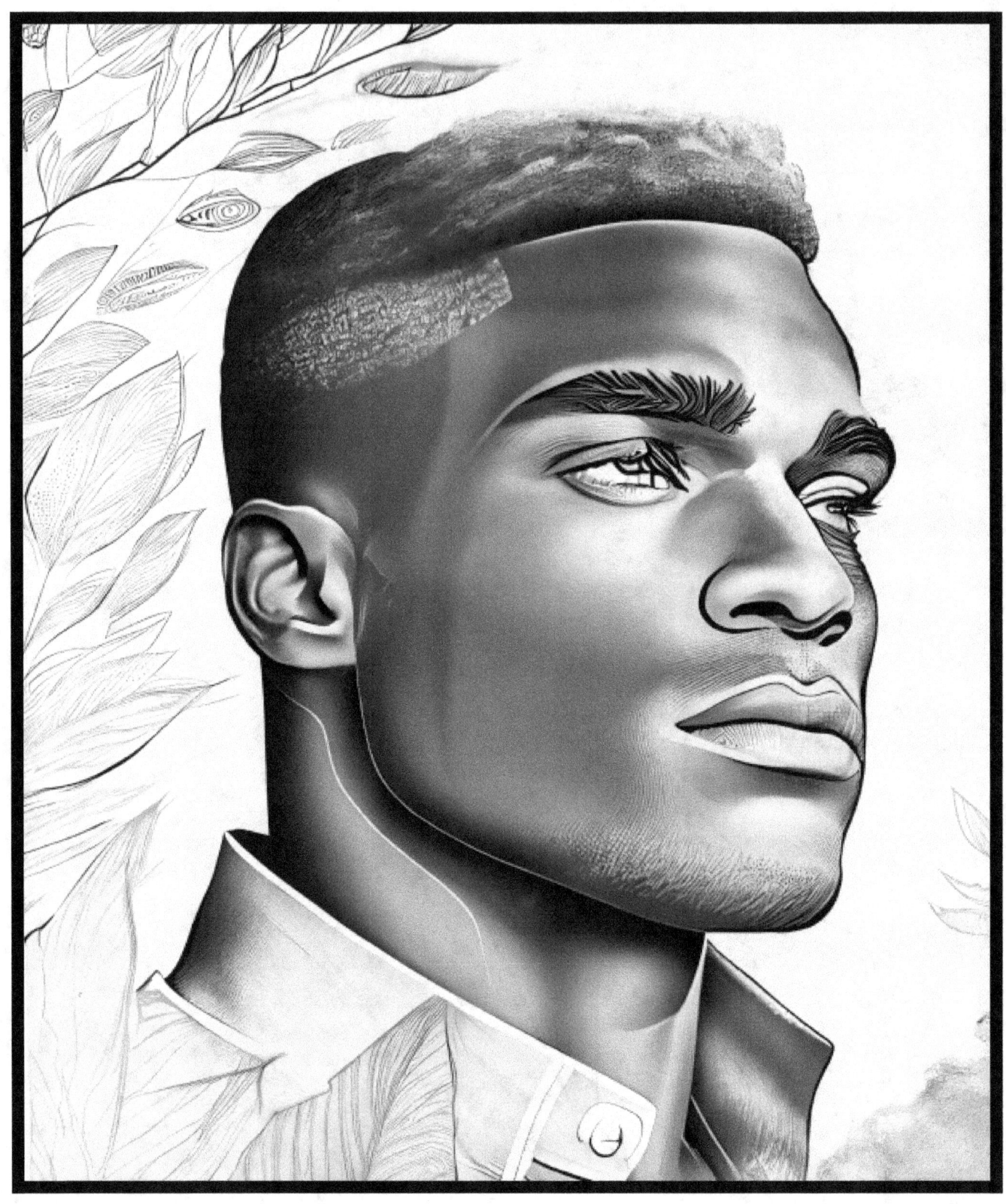

"Thoughts become things. If you see it in your mind, you will hold it in your hand." —Bob Proctor

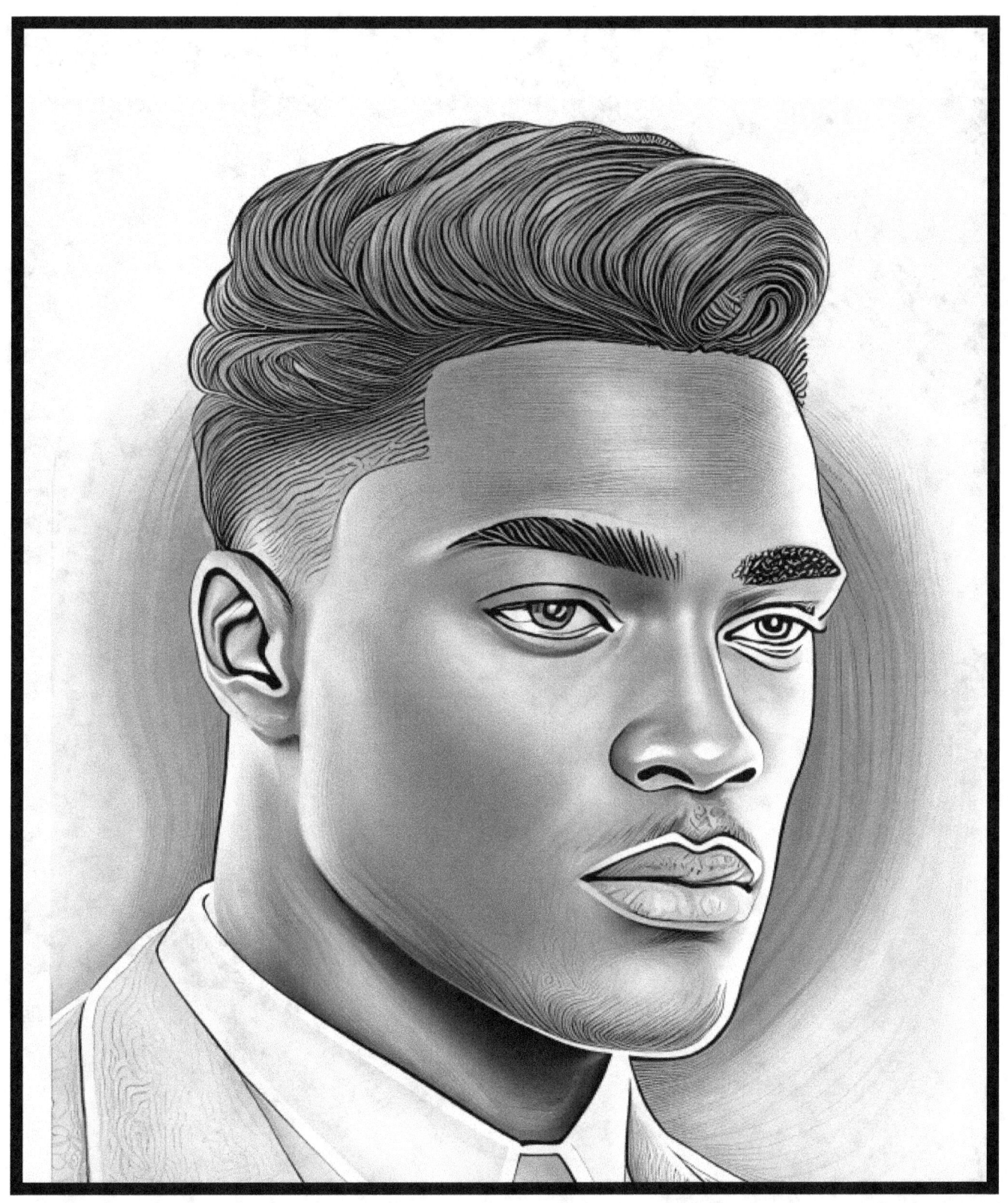

"Envision the future you desire. Create the life of your dreams. See it, feel it, believe it."
—Jack Canfield

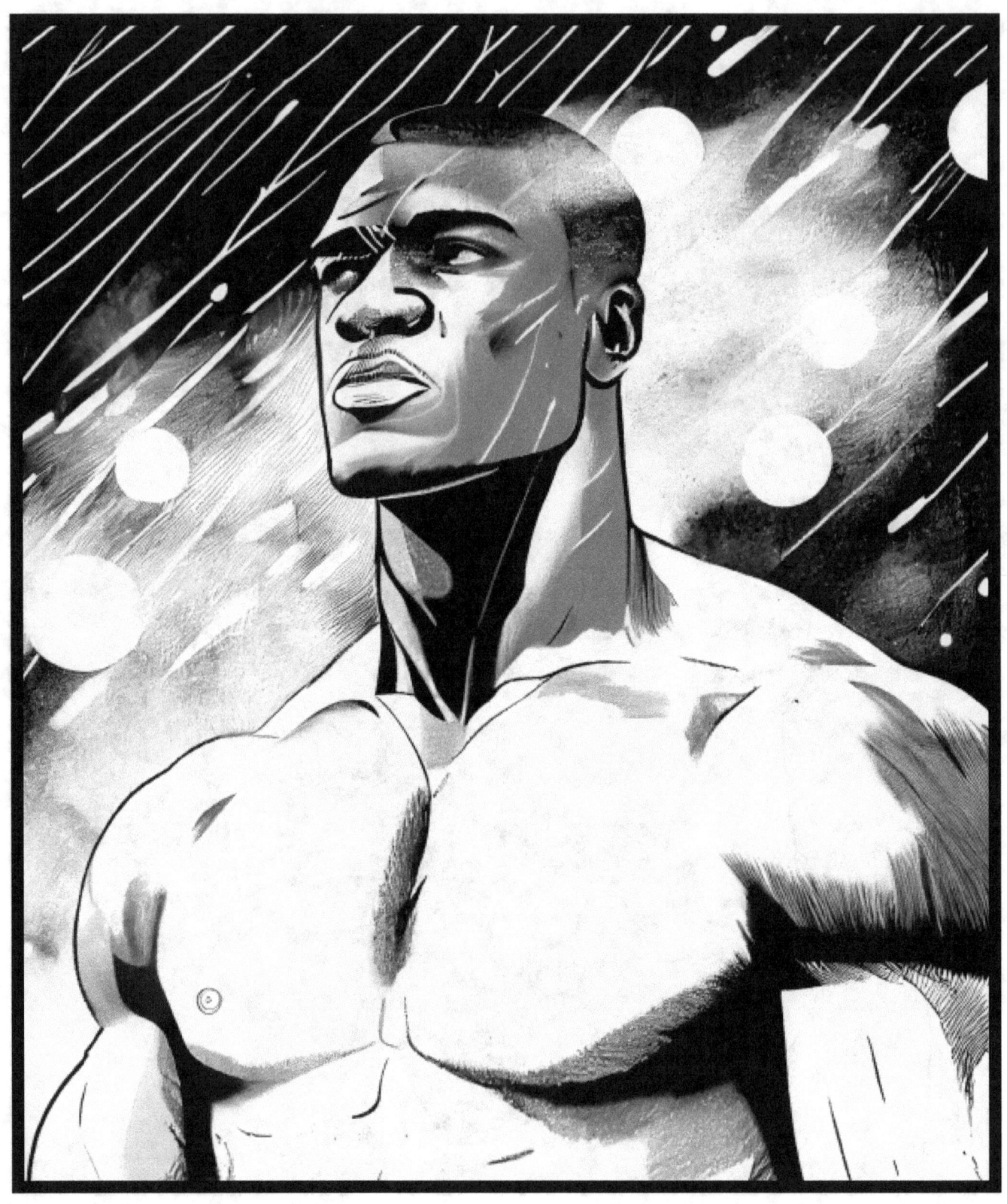

"Fully inhale your dream and completely exhale manifestation of it." —T.F. Hodge

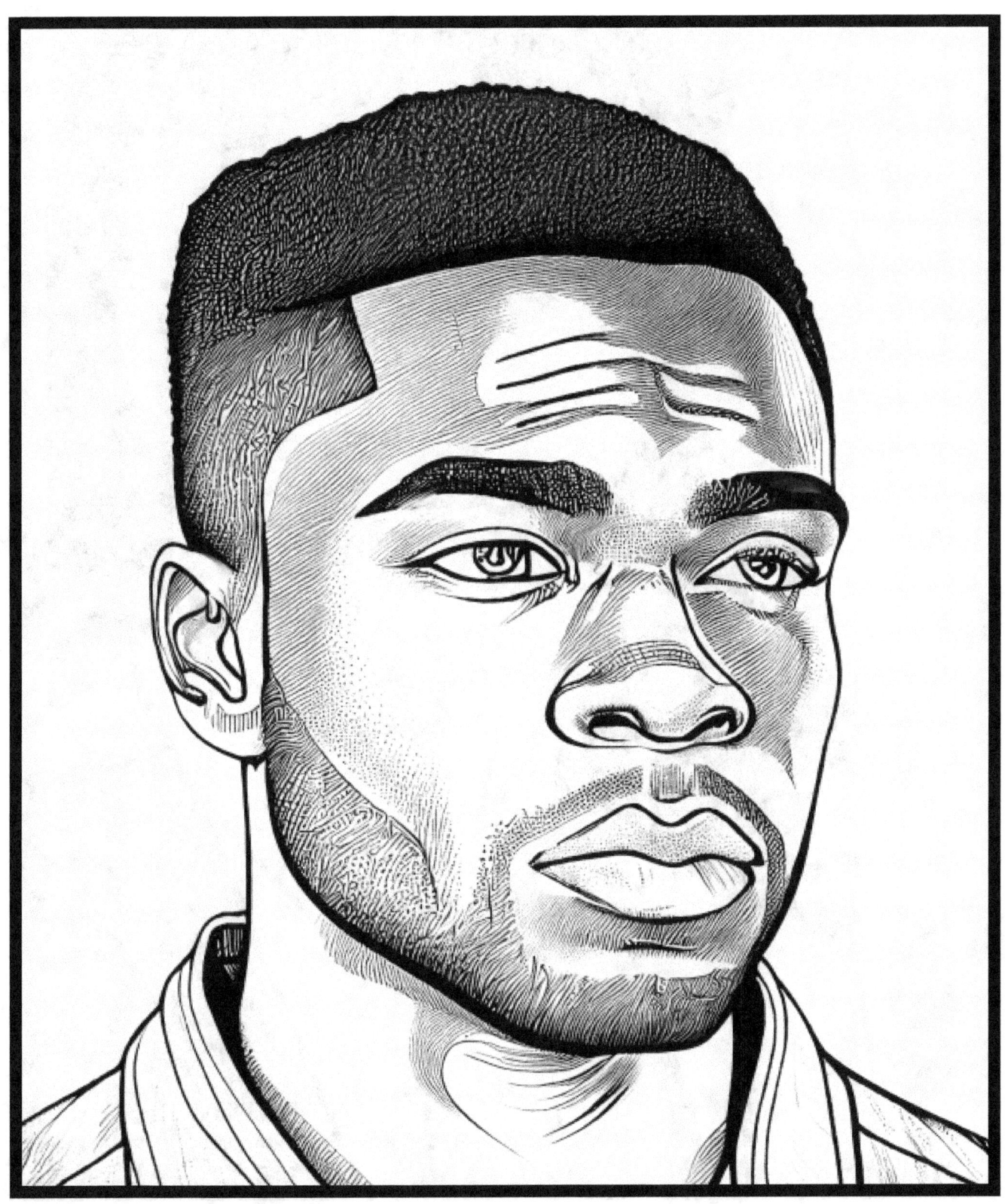

"It's unlimited what the universe can bring when you understand the great secret that thoughts become things."

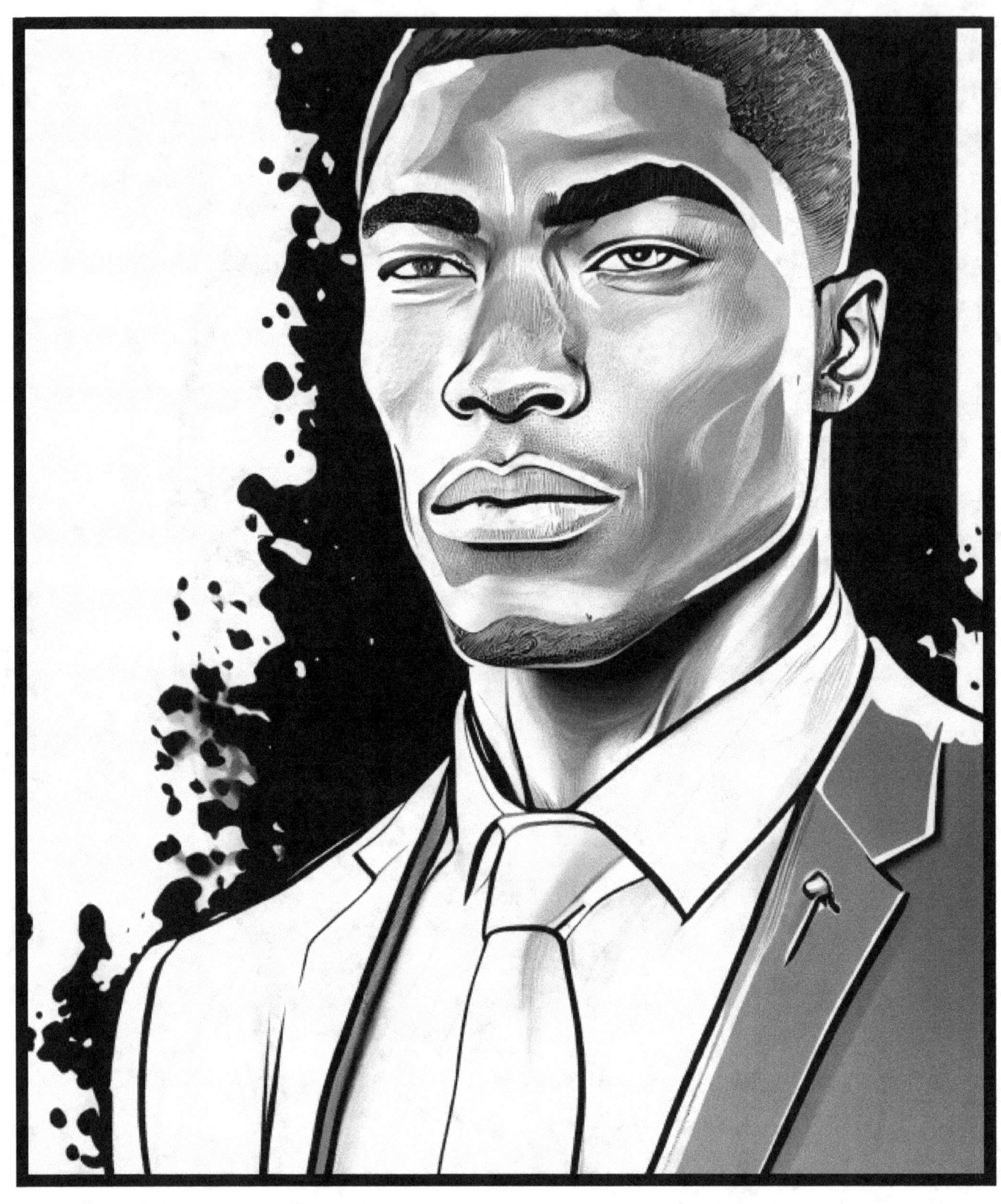

Imagination is everything. It is the preview of life's coming attractions." —Albert Einstein

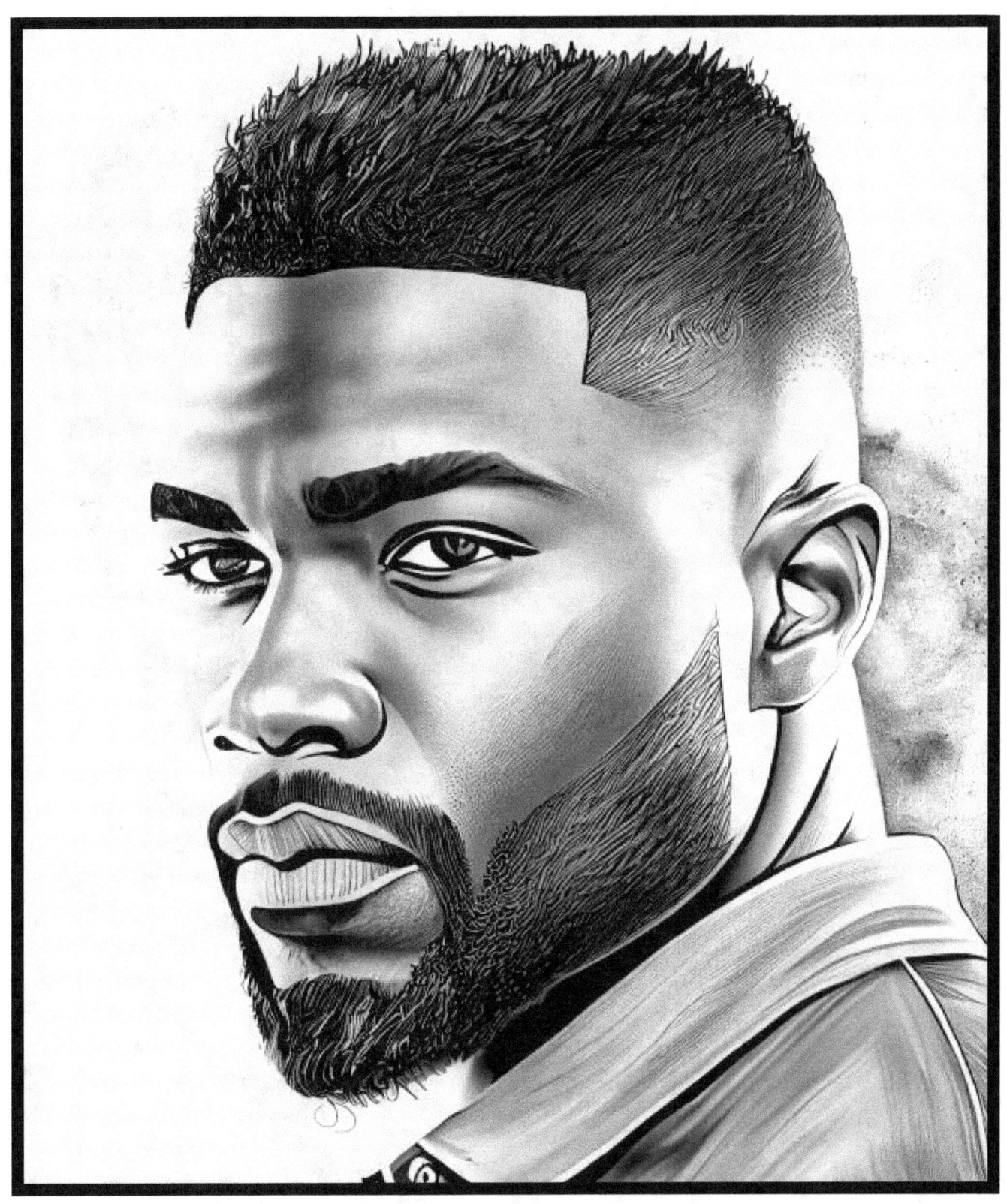

"Your time is limited. Don't waste it living someone else's life." —Steve Jobs

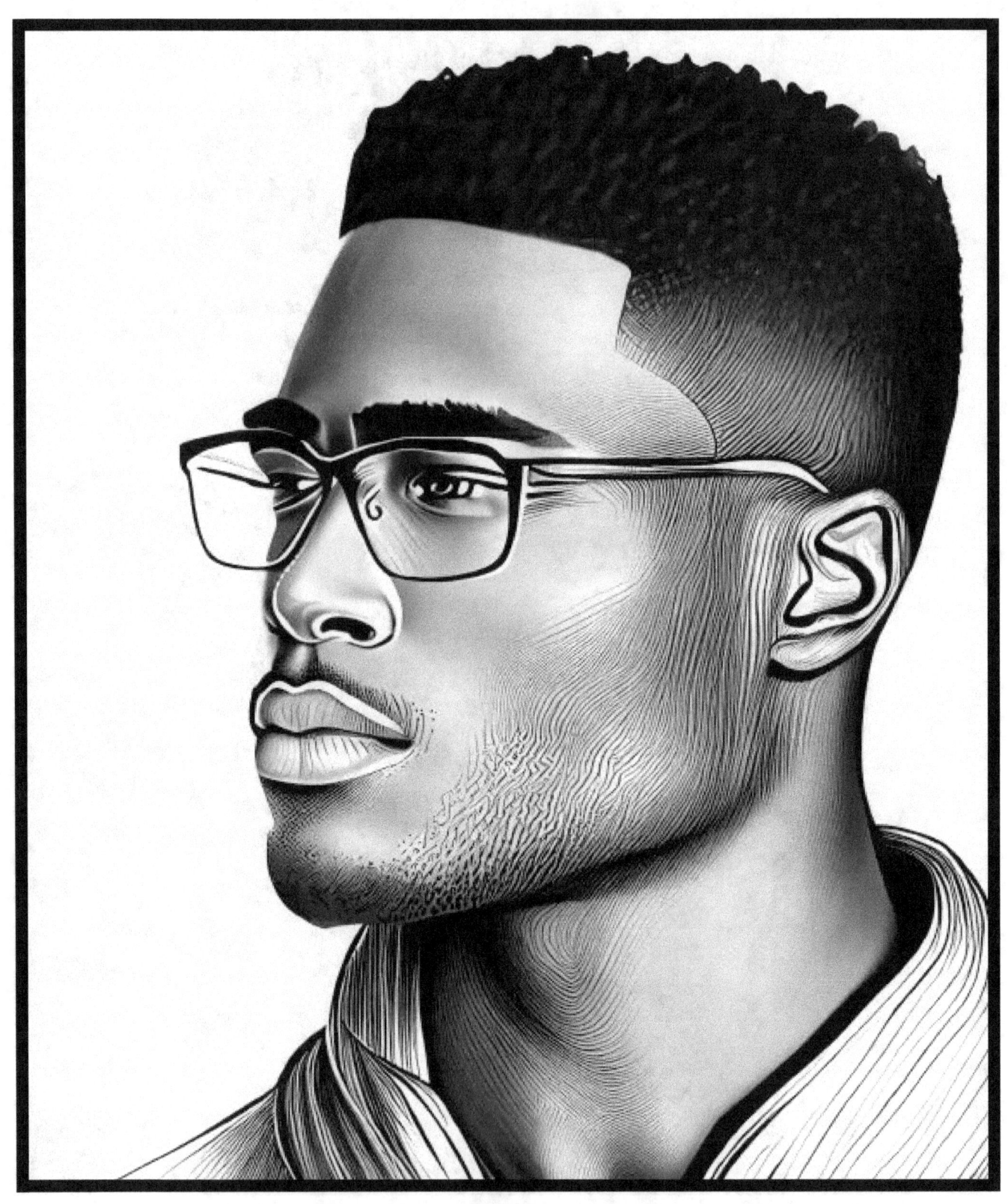

"Your mind is a powerful thing. When you fill it with positive thoughts your life will start to change."

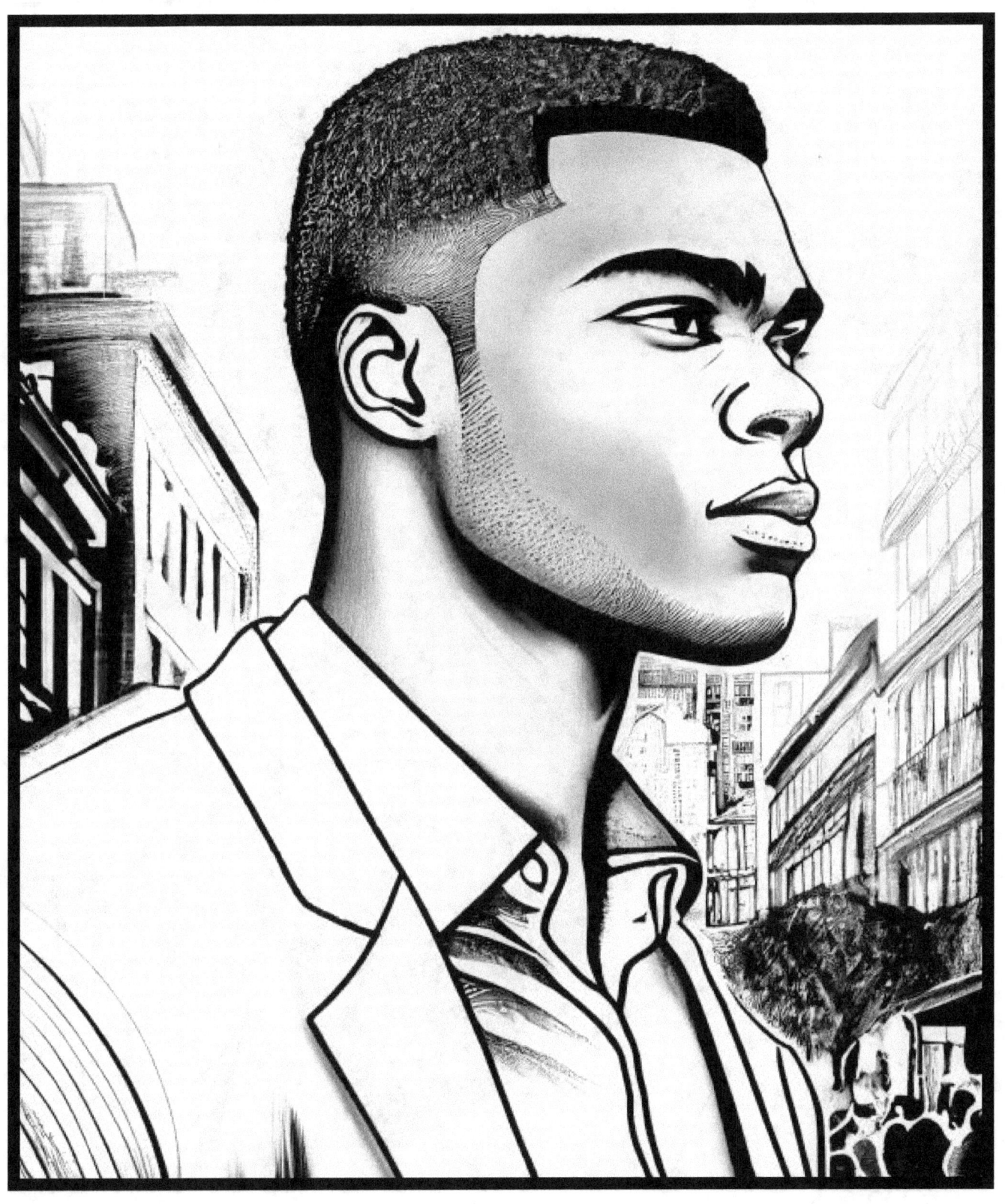

"Write it on your heart that every day is the best day in the year." —Ralph Waldo Emerson

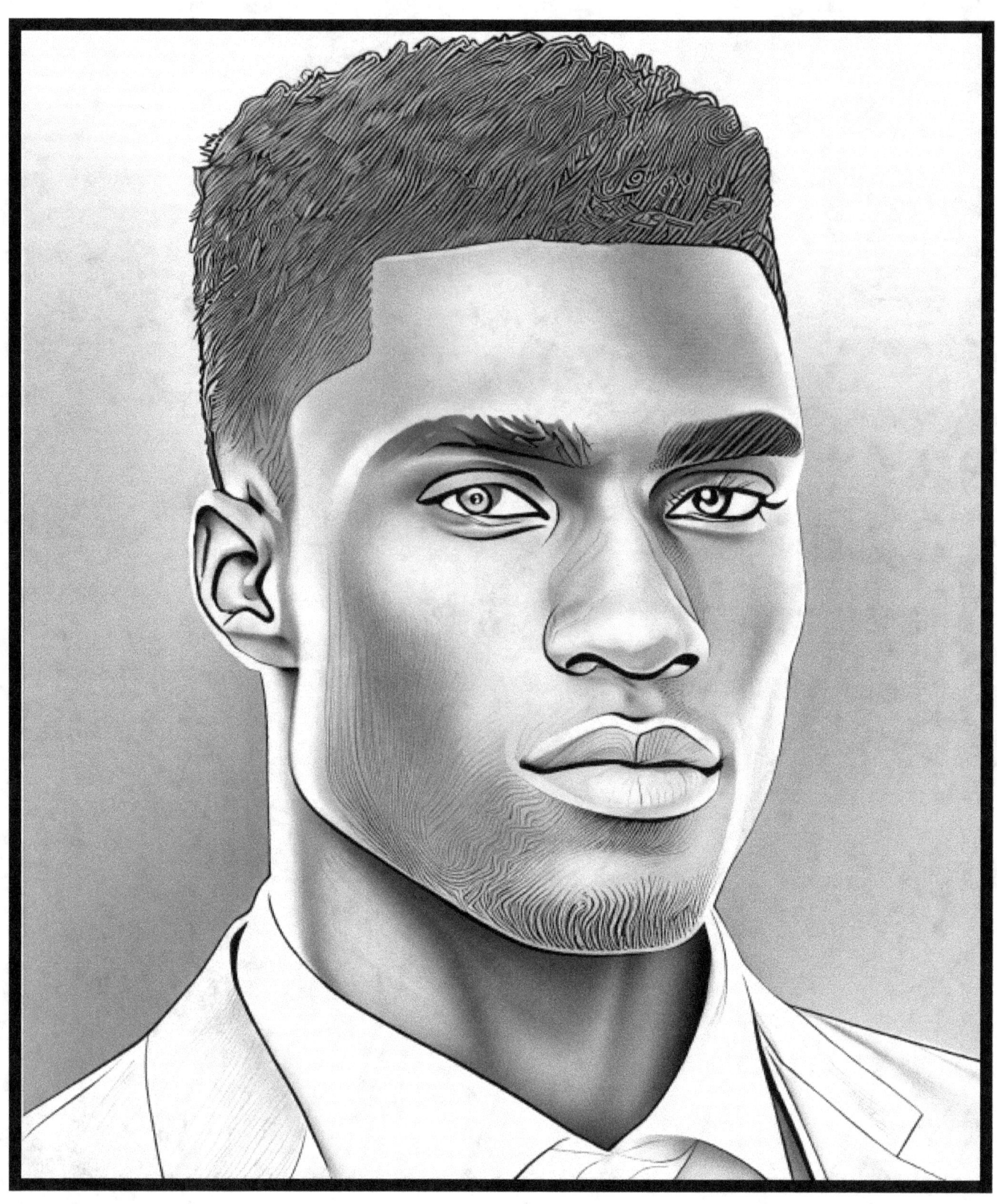

"You create your thoughts, your thoughts create your intentions, and your intentions create your reality." —Dr. Wayne Dyer

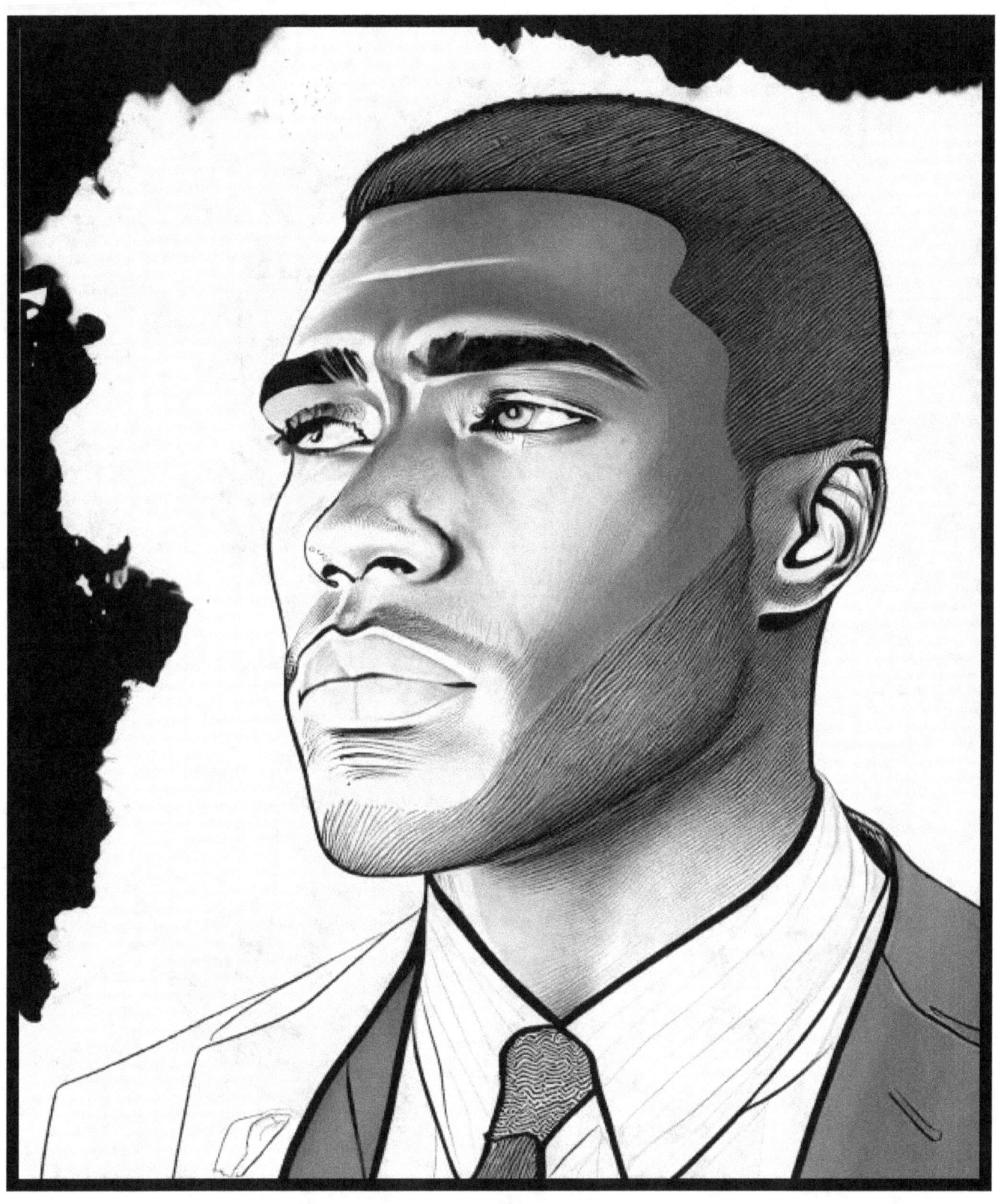

"To live your greatest life, you must first become a leader within yourself. Take charge of your life, begin attracting and manifesting all that you desire in life." —Sonia Ricotti

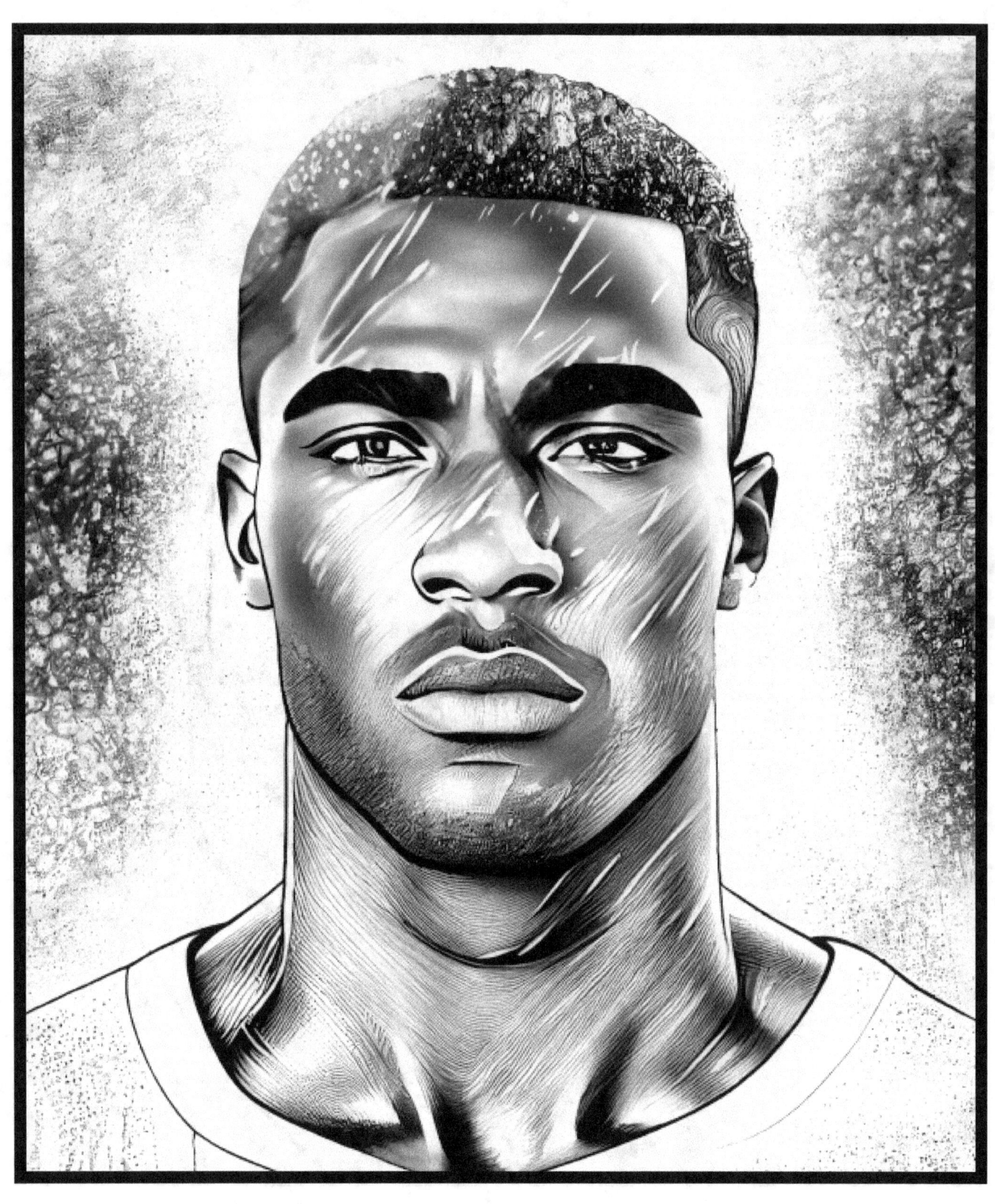

"Clarity + Alignment + Action = Manifestation."

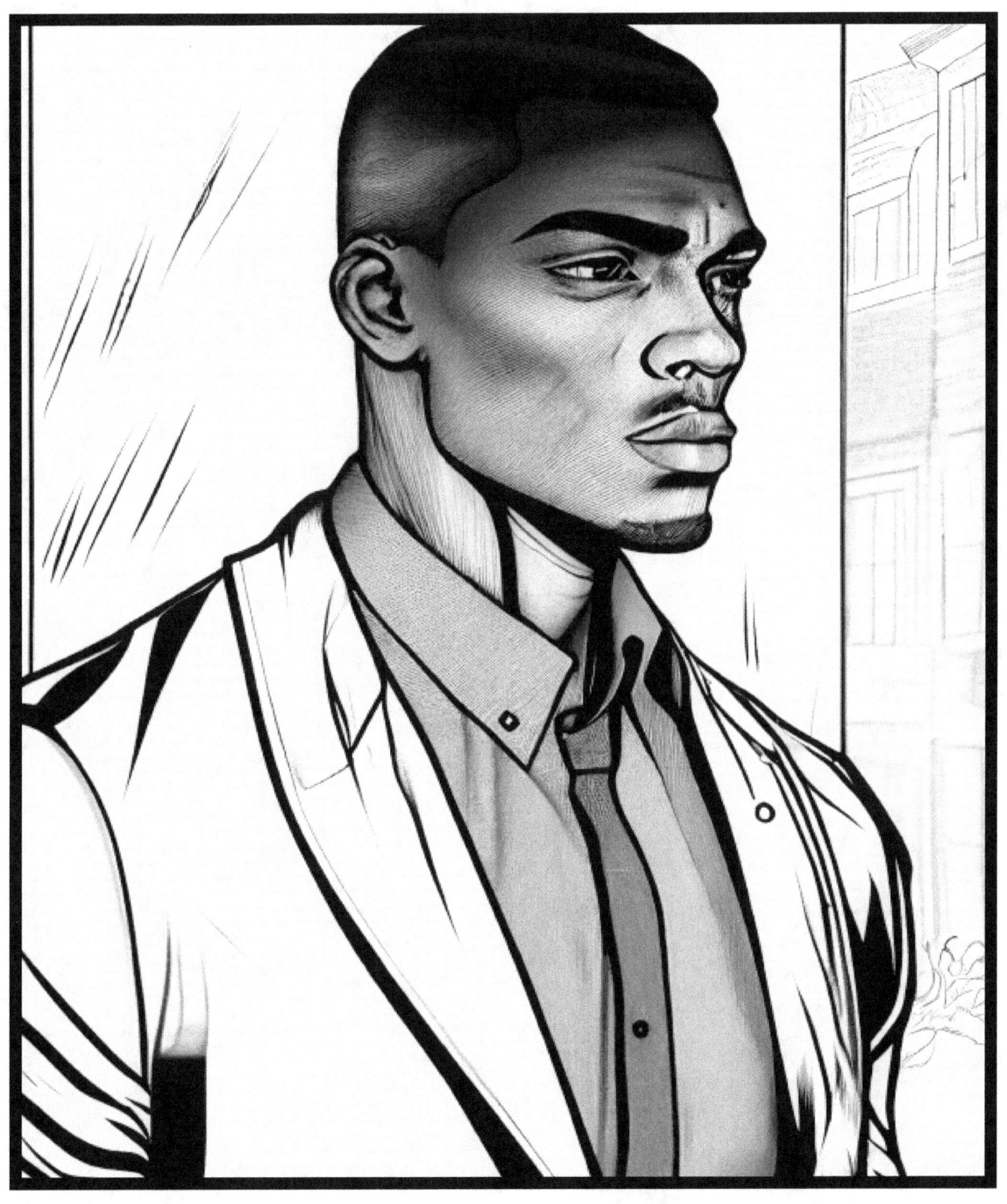

"Your mind is a powerful thing. When you fill it with positive thoughts your life will start to change."